To my cherished grandparents, Late Istalingappa Pawate and Late Gurubasappa Bhusanur, whose wisdom and unwavering devotion to Basavanna's teachings have profoundly shaped my understanding of life and spirituality.

To my beloved parents, Late Channabasappa and Late Umadevi, whose love and enduring influence have been the bedrock of my journey. Your values and teachings have guided me through every step, inspiring me to pursue knowledge and integrity.

LEADERSHIP AND CORPORATE GOVERNANCE: THE LINGAYAT WAY

CHENNAMALLIKARJUN C BHUSANUR

Contents

Contents

Contents

Preface

During my childhood, a captivating image of Basavanna hung prominently in our house, deeply influencing my thoughts and imagination. In this picture, Basavanna is depicted as a clean-shaven, well-dressed figure mounted on a horse. This image contrasts with the typical portrayal of saints and philosophical thinkers who are often shown as unkempt, bearded individuals with long hair. Instead, Basavanna appeared more like the enlightened statesman he was—a visionary leader rather than someone solely in pursuit of spiritual enlightenment.

This unique depiction of Basavanna resonated with me profoundly. To my young mind, he seemed akin to an enlightened CEO of the state, seamlessly integrating spiritual wisdom with practical governance. This perspective shaped my understanding of how ancient wisdom can be applied to modern leadership and corporate governance.

In writing this book, I am profoundly grateful for the wisdom and guidance imparted by the Lingayat tradition. The teachings of Basavanna, with their emphasis on social equality, ethical living, and personal spiritual experiences, have always captivated my heart and mind. These principles have not only shaped my values but also guided my actions and decisions. The concept of Dasoha, or selfless service, has taught me the importance of contributing to the welfare of others, while the rejection of the caste system has reinforced my commitment to equality and inclusivity.

Growing up, my grandfathers, Istalingappa Pawate and Gurubasappa Bhusanur, played a pivotal role in fueling my insatiable curiosity about matters of Lingayatism. Their wisdom, guidance, and unwavering devotion to Basavanna's principles have been a constant source of inspiration. Through countless discussions and invaluable teachings, I have come to appreciate the profound impact of Basavanna's message on our lives.

The Anubhava Mantapa, established by Basavanna, serves as a timeless example of the power of open dialogue and collective decision-making. It reminds us to listen to the voices of all individuals, regardless of their social status or background, and to value diverse perspectives. This principle has influenced my approach to leadership and collaboration, encouraging me to foster an environment where everyone's voice is heard and respected.

Incorporating Basavanna's principles into my daily life has been a journey of continuous learning and personal growth. His teachings have encouraged me to seek knowledge relentlessly and to embrace both the wisdom of the past and the possibilities of the future. This journey has enriched my understanding of the world and reinforced my dedication to living a life of integrity, service, and compassion.

My grandfathers' influence has been instrumental in deepening my connection to Lingayatism. Their dedication to Basavanna's teachings and unwavering support have inspired me to explore and engage with these principles profoundly. Through their mentorship, I have learned to appreciate the timeless relevance of Basavanna's message and to strive toward embodying these values in every aspect of my life.

In summary, the teachings of Basavanna and the essence of Lingayatism have profoundly shaped my worldview and guided my personal and spiritual journey.

This book is a testament to the enduring relevance of ancient wisdom in our contemporary world. It is my hope that this work will serve as a source of inspiration for corporate professionals, spiritual seekers, and anyone interested in the harmonious integration of tradition and modernity.

May the journey through these pages enlighten and empower you to embody the principles of "Corporate Dharma" in your professional and personal life.

With deep respect and gratitude,
Chennamallikarjun C. Bhusanur

Acknowledgements

I extend my heartfelt gratitude to my elders, relatives, teachers, and friends from my childhood and beyond. Your wisdom, support, and guidance have been the bedrock of my journey, enriching my understanding of life, dharma, and Lingayatism.

To my classmates, associates, and colleagues, your ideas and insights, whether shared in deliberate conversations or casual discussions, have been a guiding force in shaping my thoughts and forming structural ideas on various subjects. Your contributions have been invaluable, and I am deeply thankful for your influence on my work.

I must also acknowledge that I never envisioned writing a book, especially on such a profound subject. The journey of penning down my thoughts has been enlightening, and I owe a great debt of gratitude to the various online sources from which I have gained invaluable information and knowledge.

Finally, I extend my sincere thanks to the AI platforms that have assisted me in shaping this book. Your support has been instrumental in bringing this project to fruition, and I am deeply appreciative of the role you have played in this journey.

With deep respect and gratitude,
Chennamallikarjun C. Bhusanur

Prologue

An Influential Journey with Basavanna's Teachings

From an early age, the teachings of Basavanna have deeply resonated with me, capturing my interest with their timeless significance and empirical foundation. Lingayatism's core principles—social equality, ethical living, and personal spiritual experiences—have always held a special place in my heart. My grandfathers, Istalingappa Pawate and Gurubasappa Bhusanu, played a pivotal role in nurturing my curiosity about Lingayatism. Their wisdom, guidance, and unwavering devotion to Basavanna's principles were a constant source of inspiration. Through numerous discussions and invaluable teachings, I have come to understand the profound impact of Basavanna's message on our lives.

Basavanna's emphasis on ethical behavior, personal integrity, and social justice has shaped my values and guided my decisions. The concept of Dasoha, or selfless service, taught me the importance of contributing to others' welfare, while the rejection of caste reinforced my commitment to equality and inclusivity.

The Anubhava Mantapa, founded by Basavanna, exemplifies the power of open dialogue and collective decision-making. It encourages us to value diverse perspectives and listen to every voice, regardless of social status or background. This principle has influenced my approach to leadership, fostering an environment where everyone is heard and respected.

Incorporating Basavanna's teachings into my daily life has been a journey of continuous learning and growth. His principles have driven me to seek knowledge tirelessly and embrace both past wisdom and future possibilities. This journey has enriched my understanding of the world and reinforced my dedication to living a life of integrity, service, and compassion.

My grandparents' profound interest in Lingayatism further deepened my connection to its principles. Their dedication to Basavanna's teachings inspired me to explore these values deeply. Through their mentorship, I have come to appreciate the timeless relevance of Basavanna's message and strive to embody these values in all aspects of my life.

Basavanna's Teachings and Corporate Governance

Basavanna's teachings, rooted in ethical living, social equality, and personal integrity, have significant relevance in corporate governance:

Ethical Behavior: Basavanna emphasized the importance of ethics in all aspects of life. In the corporate world, this means conducting business with honesty, transparency, and integrity, which builds trust and creates a positive corporate image.

Social Equality: Basavanna's rejection of caste and advocacy for equality inspire corporations to promote diversity and inclusion. Valuing individuals based on their abilities creates a more equitable and productive work environment.

Personal Integrity: Staying true to one's values, as Basavanna taught, means corporate leaders make decisions that align with ethical standards and the long-term interests of the company and stakeholders.

Selfless Service (Dasoha): The concept of Dasoha encourages individuals to contribute to the greater good. In corporate contexts, this translates to corporate social responsibility (CSR) initiatives that give back to the community.

Open Dialogue and Collective Decision-Making (Anubhava Mantapa): The Anubhava Mantapa model promotes a culture of collaboration, where diverse perspectives are valued, and decisions are made through consensus.

By integrating Basavanna's principles, companies can enhance ethical behavior, social equality, personal integrity, selfless service, and collaborative decision-making, benefiting both corporate performance and societal well-being.

Introduction & Foundation

- *Overview of Lingayatism*

- *The Visionary Founders*

- *Harmony and Heritage: Lingayatism's Progressive Path*

CHAPTER ONE

Overview of Lingayatism

Lingayatism, founded by Basavanna in the 12th century, is a distinct religious tradition that emphasizes personal spiritual experiences, social equality, and ethical living. It emerged as a reformist movement within Hinduism, challenging the rigid caste system and ritualistic practices prevalent at the time. The Lingayats, followers of Basavanna's teachings, focus on the worship of the Ishtalinga, which represents their personal connection with the divine. They believe in the principles of Kayaka (work as worship) and Dasoha (selfless service), promoting a life of integrity, compassion, and community service.

Importance of Vachanas

The Vachanas are a collection of devotional poems written by the saints and philosophers of the Lingayat tradition, including Basavanna, Allama Prabhu, and Akka Mahadevi. These poetic verses capture the essence of Lingayat teachings and provide profound insights into spiritual and ethical living. The Vachanas emphasize direct personal experience of the divine, rejecting external rituals and intermediaries. They advocate for social equality, ethical conduct, and inner devotion. The Vachanas are significant not only as spiritual texts but also as literary treasures that reflect the rich cultural heritage of the Lingayat community. Through their powerful and evocative language, the Vachanas inspire individuals to seek truth, live ethically, and embrace inclusivity.

CHAPTER TWO

The Visionary Founders

Basavanna: The Philosopher-Saint and Statesman

Basavanna, also known as Basaveshwara, was a 12th-century philosopher, statesman, and poet who founded Lingayatism. He served as the Prime Minister of the Kalachuri dynasty in Karnataka. Basavanna's teachings emphasized social equality, ethical living, and personal spiritual experiences. He rejected the caste system and Vedic rituals, advocating for a direct and personal connection with the divine. Basavanna's concept of the Ishtalinga, a personal symbol of Shiva, symbolizes this intimate relationship with the divine. His Vachanas, poetic verses written in the Kannada language, are a profound expression of his spiritual insights and social reformist ideas.

Allama Prabhu: The Mystic Poet

Allama Prabhu was a contemporary of Basavanna and a significant figure in the Lingayat movement. He is known for his mystic poetry and deep philosophical insights. Allama Prabhu's Vachanas focus on the transcendental nature of the divine and the importance of inner spiritual experiences. His teachings emphasize the dissolution of the ego and the realization of one's true self. Allama Prabhu's profound and enigmatic verses challenge conventional religious practices and encourage seekers to look beyond external rituals to find the divine within themselves.

Akka Mahadevi: The Devotional Poetess

Akka Mahadevi was a prominent female saint and poet in the Lingayat tradition. Known for her unwavering devotion to Lord Shiva, she renounced worldly possessions and embraced a life of asceticism. Akka Mahadevi's Vachanas reflect her intense spiritual longing and her rejection of societal norms that restrict women's spiritual and social freedom. Her poetry is characterized by its passionate expression of love for the divine and its critique of social conventions. Akka Mahadevi's life and teachings continue to inspire devotion and social change, especially in the context of gender equality.

Molige Maraya: Renounced Royalness

Molige Maraya, originally known as Mahadeva Bhoopla, was a king from Kashmir who, along with his wife Ganadevi, renounced their royal life after hearing about the greatness of Basavanna. They came to Kalyana, where they adopted the simple life of a woodcutter and seller of firewood1. Maraya composed 808 vachanas (poetic expressions) under the pen name Nihkalanka Mallikarjuna, reflecting his deep philosophical, religious, and social insights. His life is a testament to the transformative power of Basavanna's teachings, showcasing the journey from royalty to a life of humility and devotion

CHAPTER THREE

Harmony and Heritage: Lingayatism's Progressive Path

Rejection of the Caste System

Lingayatism, since its inception, has been a staunch opponent of the rigid caste system that once dominated Indian society. Basavanna and his followers championed a vision of society where individuals are valued not by their birthright, but by their character and deeds. This progressive stance was revolutionary, challenging the deeply ingrained social hierarchy and promoting a new ethos of inclusivity and social justice. The principles of equality and meritocracy were central to their teachings, advocating for a society free from the shackles of caste-based discrimination.

Embracing Inclusivity and Equality

The commitment to social equality and inclusivity was a cornerstone of Lingayatism. Basavanna's establishment of the Anubhava Mantapa was a testament to this commitment. The Anubhava Mantapa was an open and inclusive forum where individuals from all walks of life—regardless of caste, gender, or social status—could come together to engage in meaningful dialogue on spiritual and social issues. This platform fostered a culture of open exchange and collective wisdom, where diverse ideas could be shared and respected. It was a pioneering model of inclusive governance and community engagement, promoting harmony and mutual respect.

Social Reforms and Their Legacy

The social reforms initiated by Basavanna and the Lingayat saints left an indelible mark on Indian society. Their relentless advocacy for social justice, gender equality, and ethical living not only addressed the immediate issues of their time but also laid the groundwork for future movements that would continue to challenge social inequalities. These progressive values resonate even today, inspiring those who seek a more just and inclusive society. The legacy of Lingayatism's social reforms is evident in various contemporary efforts towards social justice and empowerment, reflecting the enduring relevance of Basavanna's vision.

The transformative impact of Lingayatism's teachings on social structures has been profound, fostering a more equitable and compassionate society. By upholding the principles of equality, inclusivity, and ethical living, Lingayatism continues to serve as a beacon of progressive thought and social reform, offering timeless lessons for creating a harmonious and just world.

Core Teachings & Principles

- *Key Teachings of Basavanna and Their Significance to the Youth*

- *Empirical Enquiry in Basavanna's Teachings*

- *Early Life of Basavanna and His Rebellion Against Discrimination*

CHAPTER FOUR

Key Teachings of Basavanna and Their Significance to the Youth

Basavanna, born in 1131 CE in the village of Bagewadi in the Bijapur district of northern Karnataka, was destined to become a transformative figure in Indian spirituality and social reform. His parents, devout Hindus belonging to the Brahmin caste, raised him in an environment steeped in religious tradition. From a young age, Basavanna exhibited a keen intellect and a questioning mind, which set him apart from his peers.

Critical of the Caste System and Ritualistic Practices

As Basavanna grew, he became increasingly critical of the rigid caste system and the ritualistic practices that dominated popular Hinduism at the time. He observed the social injustices and inequalities perpetuated by the caste hierarchy, which granted privileges to the higher castes while marginalizing others. His sense of justice and inquisitive nature led him to challenge these norms, advocating for a more inclusive and spiritually authentic approach to life.

The Upanayana Ceremony and Basavanna's Rebellion

One pivotal event in Basavanna's early life exemplified his rebellion against caste-based discrimination and superficial rituals. The Upanayana ceremony, a significant rite of passage in Brahminical tradition, was being conducted for Basavanna. The ceremony was intended to initiate him into the spiritual life, symbolizing his readiness to study the sacred texts and perform religious duties.

During this ceremony, a profound moment of injustice deeply affected Basavanna. His sister, who was also present, was subjected to discriminatory treatment due to her gender. The Upanayana ceremony was traditionally reserved for boys, and girls were excluded from participating in this important spiritual initiation.

Witnessing this blatant discrimination against his sister, Basavanna was filled with a sense of outrage and a desire for justice. He questioned the validity and fairness of a ritual that excluded half of the population based on gender. His keen intellect and strong moral compass would not allow him to accept such an unjust practice.

In an act of defiance, Basavanna refused to undergo the Upanayana ceremony. He challenged the religious authorities and societal norms that upheld these discriminatory practices. By rejecting the ceremony, Basavanna made a powerful statement against the caste system and gender-based discrimination. His rebellion was not just an act of personal defiance but a profound declaration of his commitment to social equality and spiritual authenticity.

Impact of Basavanna's Rebellion

Basavanna's refusal to conform to the discriminatory practices of his time set the stage for his lifelong mission to promote social justice and spiritual reform. His actions demonstrated his unwavering dedication to the principles of equality and ethical living. Basavanna's rebellion against the caste system and superficial rituals inspired many others to question and challenge the status quo, laying the foundation for the broader Lingayat movement.

Basavanna's early life and his rebellion against the Upanayana ceremony highlight his courageous stand against social injustice and discrimination. His actions and teachings continue to inspire generations to strive for a more inclusive and just society, where individuals are valued based on their character and actions rather than their caste or gender. Basavanna's legacy remains a beacon of hope and a powerful reminder of the transformative power of questioning and challenging oppressive systems.

Empirical Enquiry in Basavanna's Teachings

Empirical Approach to Spirituality

Basavanna's approach to spirituality was distinctively empirical, emphasizing direct personal experience and reflection over blind adherence to rituals or dogma. This method encouraged individuals to seek and understand the divine through their own lived experiences and ethical actions, fostering a more intimate and authentic connection with their spiritual path.

Direct Experience and Personal Reflection

1. **Personal Encounter with the Divine**

   - **Living Truthfully:** Basavanna believed that the divine could be experienced directly by living truthfully and ethically. He taught that through sincere devotion, honest labor, and selfless service, individuals could attain a personal and profound experience of the divine.

- **Example**: Rather than relying solely on prescribed rituals, Basavanna advocated for the worship of Shiva through one's own actions and inner devotion, thereby making spirituality a deeply personal and accessible experience.

2. **Rejection of Blind Ritualism**

- **Critical Thinking**: Basavanna's teachings encouraged individuals to question and critically assess traditional rituals and practices. He opposed meaningless rituals that lacked personal significance or ethical grounding.
- **Example**: Basavanna's rejection of the caste system and ritualistic practices reflected his commitment to a more rational and heartfelt approach to spirituality, one that prioritizes ethical behavior and personal integrity over superficial rituals.

Resonance with Modern Quest for Knowledge

1. **Alignment with Scientific Inquiry**

- **Empirical Method**: The emphasis on empirical enquiry in Basavanna's teachings parallels the principles of scientific inquiry, where knowledge is gained through observation, experimentation, and evidence. This alignment makes his teachings particularly relevant in the modern context, where empirical evidence and rational thought are highly valued.
- **Example**: Just as scientists seek to understand the natural world through empirical methods, Basavanna

encouraged individuals to understand their spiritual world through personal experiences and ethical living.

2. **Encouraging Lifelong Learning**

    ◦ **Continuous Growth**: Basavanna's teachings promote continuous learning and personal growth. By advocating for an ongoing quest for truth and self-improvement, he inspired individuals to never cease their pursuit of knowledge and spiritual understanding.
    ◦ **Example**: The principle of Kayaka, which means work as worship, encourages individuals to engage in their duties with dedication and integrity, viewing their everyday work as a means to attain spiritual growth and fulfillment.

Ethical Living and Spiritual Fulfillment

1. **Kayaka (Work as Worship)**

    ◦ **Dedication to Duty**: Basavanna's concept of Kayaka underscores the idea that honest labor and ethical actions are forms of worship. By performing one's duties with sincerity and integrity, individuals can lead a meaningful and spiritually fulfilling life.
    ◦ **Example**: In a corporate context, this principle translates to ethical business practices, where work is conducted with honesty, transparency, and a commitment to the greater good.

2. **Dasoha (Selfless Service)**

- ◦ **Service to Others**: Dasoha emphasizes selfless service as a path to spiritual fulfillment. By serving others without expecting anything in return, individuals can cultivate a sense of compassion and interconnectedness.
- ◦ **Example**: In contemporary society, this principle can be seen in acts of community service, philanthropy, and social responsibility, where contributing to the welfare of others enriches one's own life.

Deeper Meaning and Fulfillment

1. **Inner Devotion and Ethical Conduct**

   - ◦ **Spiritual Depth**: Basavanna's teachings highlight that true spirituality is found in inner devotion and ethical conduct rather than external rituals. This approach encourages individuals to look within themselves for spiritual growth and understanding.
   - ◦ **Example**: By reflecting on their actions and striving to live ethically, individuals can find deeper meaning and fulfillment in their lives, aligning their daily practices with their spiritual beliefs.

2. **Holistic Development**

   - ◦ **Balanced Living**: The integration of ethical living, personal reflection, and direct experience creates a holistic approach to spirituality. This balance helps individuals lead a well-rounded and fulfilling life, where spiritual growth complements personal and professional development.

- **Example**: Practicing mindfulness, engaging in continuous learning, and participating in community service are ways in which individuals can embody this holistic approach in their everyday lives.

Basavanna's emphasis on empirical enquiry and direct personal experience offers a timeless and relevant approach to spirituality. By encouraging individuals to seek truth through their own experiences and ethical living, his teachings resonate with the modern quest for knowledge and understanding. This approach not only deepens one's spiritual connection but also fosters a life of integrity, compassion, and continuous growth.

CHAPTER SIX

Early Life of Basavanna and His Rebellion Against Discrimination

Basavanna, born in 1131 CE in the village of Bagewadi in the Bijapur district of northern Karnataka, was destined to become a transformative figure in Indian spirituality and social reform. His parents, devout Hindus belonging to the Brahmin caste, raised him in an environment steeped in religious tradition. From a young age, Basavanna exhibited a keen intellect and a questioning mind, which set him apart from his peers.

Critical of the Caste System and Ritualistic Practices

As Basavanna grew, he became increasingly critical of the rigid caste system and the ritualistic practices that dominated popular Hinduism at the time. He observed the social injustices and inequalities perpetuated by the caste hierarchy, which granted privileges to the higher castes while marginalizing others. His sense of justice and inquisitive nature led him to challenge these norms, advocating for a more inclusive and spiritually authentic approach to life.

The Upanayana Ceremony and Basavanna's Rebellion
One pivotal event in Basavanna's early life exemplified his rebellion against caste-based discrimination and superficial rituals. The Upanayana ceremony, a significant rite of passage in Brahminical tradition, was being conducted for Basavanna. The ceremony was intended to initiate him into the spiritual life, symbolizing his readiness to study the sacred texts and perform religious duties.

During this ceremony, a profound moment of injustice deeply affected Basavanna. His sister, who was also present, was subjected to discriminatory treatment due to her gender. The Upanayana ceremony was traditionally reserved for boys, and girls were excluded from participating in this important spiritual initiation.

Witnessing this blatant discrimination against his sister, Basavanna was filled with a sense of outrage and a desire for justice. He questioned the validity and fairness of a ritual that excluded half of the population based on gender. His keen intellect and strong moral compass would not allow him to accept such an unjust practice.

In an act of defiance, Basavanna refused to undergo the Upanayana ceremony. He challenged the religious authorities and societal norms that upheld these discriminatory practices. By rejecting the ceremony, Basavanna made a powerful statement against the caste system and gender-based discrimination. His rebellion was not just an act of personal defiance but a profound declaration of his commitment to social equality and spiritual authenticity.

Impact of Basavanna's Rebellion
Basavanna's refusal to conform to the discriminatory practices of his time set the stage for his lifelong mission to promote social justice and spiritual reform. His actions

demonstrated his unwavering dedication to the principles of equality and ethical living. Basavanna's rebellion against the caste system and superficial rituals inspired many others to question and challenge the status quo, laying the foundation for the broader Lingayat movement.

Basavanna's early life and his rebellion against the Upanayana ceremony highlight his courageous stand against social injustice and discrimination. His actions and teachings continue to inspire generations to strive for a more inclusive and just society, where individuals are valued based on their character and actions rather than their caste or gender. Basavanna's legacy remains a beacon of hope and a powerful reminder of the transformative power of questioning and challenging oppressive systems.

Contributions & Reforms of Kalyan

- *Contributions and Reforms of Basavanna*

- *Anubhava Mantapa: The Hall of Spiritual Experience*

- *Literary Works of Basavanna*

- *Legacy of Basavanna*

CHAPTER SEVEN

Contributions and Reforms of Basavanna

Rejection of Discrimination

1. Caste System Basavanna was a staunch critic of the caste system, which he viewed as an unjust and oppressive social structure. He believed that every individual, regardless of their caste, had equal worth and dignity. His teachings emphasized that true spirituality and devotion to God transcended caste boundaries. By challenging the caste system, Basavanna laid the groundwork for a more egalitarian society.

- **Example**: Basavanna's establishment of the Anubhava Mantapa was a direct challenge to the caste hierarchy. This inclusive forum welcomed individuals from all castes to participate in discussions and share their spiritual insights, promoting a culture of equality and mutual respect.

2. Class and Gender Discrimination Basavanna also opposed discrimination based on class and gender. He advocated for the upliftment of the poor and marginalized and provided a platform for women to express their spiritual experiences and contribute to the community.

- **Example**: Female saints like Akka Mahadevi were given prominence in the Lingayat movement, highlighting Basavanna's commitment to gender equality. His recognition of women's spiritual potential was revolutionary at a time when women's roles were largely confined to domestic spheres.

Introduction of the Ishtalinga

1. Symbol of Personal Devotion One of Basavanna's significant contributions was the introduction of the Ishtalinga, a personal symbol of devotion to Shiva. The Ishtalinga could be worn by anyone, regardless of their birth or social status, symbolizing the direct and personal connection each individual could have with the divine. This innovation democratized spiritual practices, making them accessible to all.

- **Symbolism**: The Ishtalinga represented the idea that divinity resides within each individual. By wearing the Ishtalinga, devotees were reminded of their direct relationship with Shiva and their own inherent spiritual potential.

2. Breaking Ritualistic Barriers The introduction of the Ishtalinga broke the monopoly of the priestly class over religious rituals. It empowered individuals to engage in personal worship and spiritual practices without intermediaries.

- **Example**: By emphasizing personal devotion over ritualistic practices, Basavanna promoted a more intimate and meaningful spiritual experience. This approach resonated with those who sought a direct connection with the divine, free from the constraints of traditional rituals and caste-based privileges.

Promotion of Ethical Living

1. Kayaka (Work as Worship) Basavanna advocated for the principle of Kayaka, which means "work as worship." He believed that performing one's duties with honesty and dedication was a form of spiritual practice. This principle emphasized the dignity of labor and the importance of ethical conduct in all aspects of life.

- **Example**: Basavanna encouraged individuals to pursue their vocations with integrity and to see their work as a means of serving society and the divine. This principle promoted a sense of responsibility and ethical behavior in professional and personal life.

2. Dasoha (Selfless Service) Another core tenet of Basavanna's teachings was Dasoha, which means "selfless service." He believed that serving others selflessly was essential for spiritual growth and fulfillment. This principle underscored the importance of compassion, generosity, and social responsibility.

- **Example**: Basavanna's emphasis on Dasoha inspired the establishment of community kitchens and other charitable activities, fostering a culture of service and mutual support within the Lingayat community.

Significance and Legacy

1. Social Reforms Basavanna's socio-religious reforms had a profound and lasting impact on Indian society. His advocacy for social justice, gender equality, and ethical living laid the foundation for future movements that sought to address social inequalities. His teachings continue to inspire efforts towards creating a more just and inclusive society.

- **Example**: The Lingayat movement, which emerged from Basavanna's teachings, played a crucial role in challenging and transforming oppressive social structures. It promoted a vision of society based on equality, justice, and compassion.

2. Spiritual and Cultural Heritage The introduction of the Ishtalinga and the principles of Kayaka and Dasoha remain central to the spiritual and cultural heritage of the Lingayat community. These contributions have enriched the spiritual landscape of India and continue to guide the ethical and spiritual practices of millions of people.

- **Example**: The continued reverence for the Ishtalinga and the emphasis on ethical living and selfless service in the Lingayat community highlight the enduring relevance of Basavanna's teachings.

Basavanna's transformative contributions and reforms were pivotal in creating a more inclusive and just society. His rejection of caste, class, and gender discrimination, along with the introduction of the Ishtalinga, promoted social equality and personal devotion. His principles of Kayaka and Dasoha emphasized ethical living and selfless service, leaving a lasting legacy that continues to inspire and guide people today.

CHAPTER EIGHT

Anubhava Mantapa: The Hall of Spiritual Experience

Basavanna's establishment of the **Anubhava Mantapa** was a groundbreaking initiative that transformed the socio-religious landscape of his time. Known as the "Hall of Spiritual Experience," the Anubhava Mantapa served as a revolutionary forum where individuals from all walks of life could come together to engage in open and inclusive dialogue on spiritual and worldly matters. Here's an elaboration on its significance and impact:

Inclusivity and Open Dialogue

Breaking Barriers of Caste and Social Status

- **Social Equality**: The Anubhava Mantapa was founded on the principle of social equality, promoting the idea that every individual, regardless of their caste, class, or gender, had a right to participate in spiritual and intellectual discourse. This inclusivity was revolutionary, as it challenged the deeply entrenched social hierarchies of the time.

- **Example**: By welcoming people from diverse backgrounds, including lower castes and women, the Anubhava Mantapa broke down barriers that had long divided society. It provided a platform for marginalized voices to be heard and respected.

Encouraging Intellectual Exchange

- **Open Forum**: The Anubhava Mantapa was designed as an open forum where participants could freely discuss and debate a wide range of topics, from spiritual philosophy to social justice. This environment encouraged the exchange of ideas and collective wisdom, fostering a culture of intellectual growth and innovation.
- **Example**: The dialogues and debates that took place at the Anubhava Mantapa were documented in the form of Vachanas, which encapsulated the teachings and insights shared by various participants. These writings continue to be a valuable source of spiritual and philosophical knowledge.

Promoting Ethical and Rational Living
Empirical Enquiry and Rational Thought

- **Seeking Truth**: Basavanna encouraged participants at the Anubhava Mantapa to seek truth through empirical enquiry and personal experience. He emphasized the importance of rational thought and critical thinking in spiritual practices.
- **Example**: The focus on empirical enquiry and rationality resonated with many individuals who sought a more meaningful and authentic spiritual path, free

from the constraints of ritualistic practices and superstitions.

Ethical Principles

- **Kayaka and Dasoha**: The Anubhava Mantapa promoted Basavanna's principles of Kayaka (work as worship) and Dasoha (selfless service). These ethical guidelines emphasized the importance of honest labor and selfless service as key components of a spiritually fulfilling life.
- **Example**: Participants at the Anubhava Mantapa were encouraged to engage in their respective vocations with dedication and integrity, while also contributing to the welfare of others through acts of service and generosity.

Impact and Legacy
Social Reforms

- **Challenging Social Norms**: The Anubhava Mantapa played a crucial role in challenging and transforming oppressive social norms. By advocating for social equality and ethical living, it laid the foundation for broader socio-religious reforms that sought to address injustices and inequalities.
- **Example**: The inclusive and egalitarian principles of the Anubhava Mantapa inspired future movements that aimed to create a more just and equitable society. Its legacy continues to influence contemporary efforts toward social justice and empowerment.

Spiritual and Cultural Heritage

- **Continued Relevance**: The teachings and practices that emerged from the Anubhava Mantapa have had a lasting impact on the spiritual and cultural heritage of the Lingayat community. The emphasis on inclusivity, open dialogue, and ethical living remains central to the community's values and practices.
- **Example**: The enduring reverence for the Anubhava Mantapa and its principles is evident in the continued emphasis on personal devotion, social equality, and rational spirituality within the Lingayat tradition.

The Anubhava Mantapa, established by Basavanna, was a transformative institution that promoted inclusivity, open dialogue, and ethical living. By breaking down the barriers of caste and social status, it created a forum where diverse voices could be heard and respected. Its emphasis on empirical enquiry and rational thought, combined with the principles of Kayaka and Dasoha, fostered a culture of intellectual and spiritual growth. The legacy of the Anubhava Mantapa continues to inspire efforts toward social justice, equality, and a more meaningful spiritual life.

CHAPTER NINE

Basavanna's establishment of the Anubhava Mantapa was a groundbreaking initiative.

Introduction to Vachanas

Basavanna's literary genius is most prominently reflected in his Vachanas, a distinctive form of poetic prose written in Kannada. These Vachanas are characterized by their simplicity and directness, yet they encapsulate profound spiritual, ethical, and social teachings. Basavanna's ability to communicate complex ideas in an accessible manner made his Vachanas resonate with a broad audience, transcending social and cultural boundaries.

Themes and Messages

1. Spiritual Teachings

- **Personal Devotion**: Basavanna's Vachanas emphasize the importance of personal devotion and a direct relationship with the divine. He advocated for an inner spiritual journey, encouraging individuals to seek the divine within themselves rather than through external rituals.
- **Example**: A Vachana might express the idea that true worship comes from the heart and soul, rather than through elaborate ceremonies. This message empowers individuals to find spiritual fulfillment in their everyday actions and thoughts.

2. Ethical Living

- **Integrity and Honesty**: Basavanna's teachings on ethical living are a recurring theme in his Vachanas. He emphasized the principles of Kayaka (work as worship) and Dasoha (selfless service), urging people to live with integrity, honesty, and a sense of responsibility.
- **Example**: Through his Vachanas, Basavanna conveyed that ethical behavior and sincere devotion are the true paths to spiritual enlightenment. He criticized those who performed religious rituals without ethical conduct, highlighting the importance of aligning one's actions with one's beliefs.

3. Social Justice

- **Rejection of Caste and Gender Discrimination**: Basavanna was a fierce advocate for social equality. His Vachanas often criticize the rigid caste system and gender discrimination, promoting the idea that all individuals are equal in the eyes of the divine.

- **Example**: In his Vachanas, Basavanna denounced the social hierarchies that marginalized certain groups and called for a society where everyone is treated with dignity and respect, regardless of their birth or social status.

4. Critique of Superficial Rituals

- **Rational Spirituality**: Basavanna's Vachanas often criticize meaningless rituals and superstitions. He encouraged a more rational and heartfelt approach to spirituality, where inner devotion and ethical living took precedence over external practices.
- **Example**: A Vachana might illustrate the futility of rituals performed without genuine devotion, urging individuals to focus on inner spiritual growth and ethical conduct instead.

Impact and Legacy
1. Foundation of Lingayat Literature

- **Cultural Heritage**: Basavanna's Vachanas have become a cornerstone of Lingayat literature, deeply influencing the spiritual and cultural identity of the Lingayat community. They are treasured not only for their literary beauty but also for their profound messages of social reform and personal devotion.
- **Example**: The Vachanas continue to be recited, studied, and revered by Lingayats, serving as a source of inspiration and guidance for personal and communal life.

2. Inspiration for Social Reform

- **Advocacy for Equality**: The social and ethical teachings in Basavanna's Vachanas have inspired countless generations to advocate for a more just and egalitarian society. His emphasis on equality, rationality, and ethical living has left a lasting impact on social reform movements.
- **Example**: Activists and reformers have drawn on Basavanna's teachings to challenge social injustices and promote inclusive policies that reflect his vision of a society based on equality and compassion.

3. Influence on Kannada Literature

- **Literary Innovation**: Basavanna's innovative use of the Kannada language in his Vachanas set a precedent for future literary works. His style of poetic prose, characterized by its clarity and depth, has influenced numerous writers and poets in Kannada literature.
- **Example**: The simplicity and directness of Basavanna's Vachanas have inspired modern Kannada poets and writers to explore themes of spirituality, ethics, and social justice in their works.

Basavanna's Vachanas are a testament to his literary brilliance and his commitment to social and spiritual reform. Their simplicity belies the depth of their teachings, which address a wide range of issues from personal devotion and ethical living to social justice and rational spirituality. As a cornerstone of Lingayat literature, Basavanna's Vachanas continue to inspire and guide countless individuals, leaving an indelible mark on both spiritual practice and social thought.

CHAPTER TEN

Legacy of Basavanna

Enduring Impact on Indian Society

1. Influence in Karnataka Basavanna's teachings and socio-religious reforms have left a profound and lasting impact on Indian society, particularly in the state of Karnataka. His visionary ideas and transformative actions continue to shape the cultural and spiritual landscape of the region.

- **Cultural Heritage**: Basavanna's contributions are deeply woven into the cultural fabric of Karnataka. His teachings have been integrated into various aspects of daily life, influencing everything from social customs to spiritual practices.
- **Example**: The annual Basava Jayanti, celebrated with great fervor in Karnataka, commemorates Basavanna's birth and his enduring contributions to society. It is a day of reflection on his teachings and their relevance to contemporary issues.

Principles of Social Equality

2. Rejection of Caste Discrimination One of Basavanna's most significant legacies is his staunch opposition to caste-based discrimination. By advocating for social equality, he challenged the deeply entrenched caste hierarchy and promoted the idea that all individuals are equal in the eyes of the divine.

- **Social Reforms**: His efforts to dismantle the caste system laid the groundwork for future social reform movements. The principles of equality and inclusivity that he championed continue to inspire efforts to address social injustices and promote a more equitable society.
- **Example**: Modern movements for social justice and caste equity in India often draw upon Basavanna's teachings, highlighting the timeless relevance of his advocacy for equality.

Promotion of Ethical Living

3. Ethical Conduct and Personal Devotion Basavanna emphasized the importance of ethical living and personal devotion. His teachings on Kayaka (work as worship) and Dasoha (selfless service) have become guiding principles for living a life of integrity and compassion.

- **Work Ethic**: The concept of Kayaka encourages individuals to perform their duties with dedication and honesty, viewing work as a form of worship. This principle has influenced various professional and personal domains, promoting a strong work ethic and ethical conduct.
- **Example**: In contemporary corporate governance, the principles of ethical conduct and social responsibility echo Basavanna's teachings on Kayaka and Dasoha, emphasizing the need for integrity and community service in business practices.

Fostering Inclusivity

4. Inclusivity and Open Dialogue The establishment of the Anubhava Mantapa by Basavanna was a pioneering effort to foster inclusivity and open dialogue. This forum allowed individuals from diverse backgrounds to engage in meaningful discussions on spiritual and social matters, breaking down barriers of caste and social status.

- **Collective Wisdom**: The inclusive nature of the Anubhava Mantapa promoted collective wisdom and mutual respect, encouraging a culture of dialogue and intellectual growth.
- **Example**: Modern initiatives that aim to create inclusive platforms for discussion and collaboration, such as community forums and think tanks, reflect the principles of the Anubhava Mantapa, promoting inclusivity and shared learning.

Vibrant Lingayat Community

5. Living Legacy Through Lingayat Community Basavanna's teachings continue to thrive through the vibrant Lingayat community. The values and principles he championed remain central to the community's identity and practices, guiding their spiritual and social lives.

- **Spiritual Practices**: The Ishtalinga, introduced by Basavanna, remains a cherished symbol of personal devotion for Lingayats. It represents the direct and personal connection between the individual and the divine.
- **Example**: Lingayat literature, festivals, and daily rituals are deeply influenced by Basavanna's teachings, ensuring that his legacy remains a living and dynamic

force in the community.

Enduring Influence of Vachanas

6. Literary Contributions The Vachanas of Basavanna have become a cornerstone of Lingayat literature, inspiring countless generations with their profound spiritual and ethical teachings. These poetic expressions continue to resonate with people, offering guidance and inspiration for living a meaningful and principled life.

- **Cultural Significance**: The Vachanas are not only literary treasures but also serve as a source of moral and spiritual guidance. They encapsulate Basavanna's vision of a just and compassionate society, where personal devotion and ethical living are paramount.
- **Example**: Scholars, poets, and spiritual leaders continue to study and draw inspiration from the Vachanas, ensuring that Basavanna's teachings remain relevant and influential in contemporary discourse.

Basavanna's legacy is a testament to the enduring power of his teachings on social equality, ethical living, and rational spirituality. His principles continue to resonate with people today, inspiring ongoing social and spiritual progress. The vibrant Lingayat community and the enduring influence of his Vachanas ensure that Basavanna's transformative impact remains a guiding light for future generations.

Key Figures & Their Impact

- *Sharane Sri Danamma Devi: A Revered Figure in Lingayatism*

- *Channabasavanna'; A limunary of Lingayatism*

- *Allam Prabhu: A Luminary of Lingayatism*

Sharane Sri Danamma Devi: A Revered Figure in Lingayatism

Sharane Sri Danamma Devi, also known as Guddapur Danamma Devi, is a highly respected and venerated figure in Lingayatism. Her life and contributions embody the principles of devotion, service, and equality that are central to the faith. Here are the key details about her life and legacy:

Early Life
Birth and Naming

- **Birth:** Danamma Devi was born as Lingamma Umarani in the village of Umarani, located in Maharashtra. From an early age, she exhibited a deep spiritual inclination and a strong sense of devotion. Her innate spirituality set her apart, and she was recognized for her dedication to her faith from a young age.
- **Naming by Basavanna:** It was Jagajyoti Basavanna, the revered founder of Lingayatism, who recognized her spiritual potential and renamed her Danamma. He

foretold that she would be worshipped worldwide, acknowledging her future significance in the spiritual realm. This recognition by Basavanna was a turning point in her life, setting the stage for her future spiritual contributions.

Spiritual Calling

- **Early Signs**: From a young age, Danamma Devi displayed a profound spiritual calling. She was deeply committed to her faith and showed a remarkable understanding of spiritual principles, which set her apart from her peers. Her early life was marked by acts of devotion and a deep connection to the divine.
- **Divine Prophecy**: The prophecy by Basavanna that she would be worshipped globally became a guiding light in her life, encouraging her to devote herself fully to spiritual and community service. This prophecy gave her a sense of purpose and direction, motivating her to live a life dedicated to serving others and spreading the teachings of Lingayatism.

Contributions
Community Service

- **Acts of Charity**: Danamma Devi was renowned for her acts of charity and service to the community. She was dedicated to solving people's problems and providing for the needy. Her compassionate nature and selfless actions earned her immense respect and devotion from her followers. She was known for her unwavering commitment to helping those in distress and for her generous spirit.

- **Support to the Needy**: She actively engaged in helping those in distress, offering food, shelter, and assistance to anyone in need. Her unwavering commitment to service reflected the core Lingayat principle of Dasoha (selfless service). Her acts of charity were not just about providing material support but also about offering emotional and spiritual guidance to those in need.

Spreading Teachings

- **Promoting Lingayat Principles**: Danamma Devi traveled extensively, spreading the teachings of Basavanna and promoting the core principles of Lingayatism. She played a crucial role in educating people about the values of devotion, equality, and ethical living. Her travels and teachings helped to spread the message of Lingayatism far and wide, reaching people from all walks of life.
- **Inspiring Devotion**: Through her teachings and personal example, she inspired countless individuals to embrace the spiritual path and live a life of integrity and devotion. Her ability to connect with people and convey spiritual principles in an accessible and relatable way made her an influential spiritual leader.

Miracles

- **Miraculous Deeds**: Danamma Devi is believed to have performed many miracles, which further solidified her status as a revered spiritual figure. These miracles often involved helping those in need and fulfilling the wishes of her devotees, enhancing their faith and devotion. Stories of her miraculous deeds have been passed down through generations, adding to her legendary status.

- **Divine Interventions**: Stories of her miraculous interventions have been passed down through generations, contributing to her legendary status within the Lingayat community. These stories serve as a testament to her spiritual power and her deep connection to the divine.

Legacy
Guddapur Temple

- **Temple Erection**: After her aikya (union with the divine), a temple was erected in her honor in Guddapur, Sangli District, Maharashtra. This temple has become a significant pilgrimage site, attracting devotees from all over. It serves as a place of worship and a testament to her lasting impact on the community.
- **Place of Worship**: The Guddapur Temple serves as a center of worship and a testament to her lasting impact on the community. Devotees visit the temple to seek her blessings and to honor her contributions. The temple is a place of spiritual solace and a symbol of her enduring influence.

Worship and Devotion

- **Incarnation of Goddess Parvati**: Danamma Devi is worshipped as an incarnation of Goddess Parvati. Devotees believe in her ability to fulfill their wishes and provide divine guidance. Her life and work continue to inspire devotion and service within the Lingayat community.

- **Continuing Influence**: Her life and work continue to inspire devotion and service within the Lingayat community. She remains a symbol of the enduring values of Lingayatism, including devotion, service, and equality. Her teachings and example continue to guide and inspire new generations of devotees.

Danamma Devi's life and contributions are celebrated for their embodiment of the principles of Lingayatism. She stands as a shining example of selfless service, spiritual devotion, and unwavering commitment to equality.

CHAPTER TWELVE

Channabasavanna: A luminary Sharana

The influence of Channabasavanna on the Sharana movement is immense

1. Siddharameshwar

- **Influence**: Siddharameshwar was a male Sharana deeply influenced by the teachings of Channabasavanna. Known for his spiritual purity and unwavering commitment to the principles of Lingayatism, he played a significant role in the Lingayat movement.
- **Legacy**: His devotion and adherence to the spiritual and ethical teachings of Lingayatism have left an enduring legacy. Siddharameshwar's life and works continue to inspire devotees, emphasizing the importance of spiritual integrity and purity.

2. Lakshmidevi

- **Contributions**: Lakshmidevi was a prominent female Sharana who significantly contributed to the spiritual and cultural heritage of Lingayatism. Her Vachanas are celebrated for their poetic elegance and profound spiritual depth.

- **Impact**: Lakshmidevi's writings reflect her deep spiritual insights and her commitment to the principles of devotion, equality, and ethical living. Her works continue to be revered, providing inspiration and guidance to many within the Lingayat community.

Legacy and Impact of Female Sharanas

These female Sharanas played a crucial role in shaping the spiritual and cultural landscape of Lingayatism. Their contributions, through their Vachanas and their exemplary lives, continue to inspire and guide devotees. They are remembered for their unwavering devotion, their spiritual insights, and their commitment to the principles of equality and inclusivity. By breaking societal norms and contributing significantly to spiritual discourse, they paved the way for future generations to follow in their footsteps.

Akkamahadevi: A Prominent Poet and Saint
Early Life

- **Birth**: Akka Mahadevi was born in 1130 CE in Udutadi, near Shivamogga, Karnataka. From an early age, she exhibited a deep spiritual inclination and devotion to Lord Shiva.
- **Family**: Born into a Kannada-speaking family, she was married at a young age to a local chieftain named Kausika. However, her marital life was short-lived due to her unwavering devotion to Lord Shiva, which led her to renounce worldly ties.

Spiritual Journey

- **Devotion to Shiva**: Akka Mahadevi's spiritual journey began with her deep devotion to Lord Shiva. She renounced her worldly life and became a wandering ascetic, seeking spiritual enlightenment. Her dedication to Shiva was profound, often referring to herself as Shiva's bride.
- **Poetry and Philosophy**: She composed many Vachanas (poetic expressions) that reflect her spiritual experiences and philosophical thoughts. Her poetry is known for its simplicity, depth, and emotional intensity, making her one of the most celebrated poets in Kannada literature.

Literary Contributions

- **Vachanas**: Akka Mahadevi's Vachanas are an integral part of Kannada literature. They are characterized by their lyrical beauty and profound spiritual insights, capturing the essence of her devotion and philosophical musings.
- **Themes**: Her poetry often explores themes of love, devotion, and the soul's quest for union with the divine. Her works convey a deep sense of spiritual longing and the transcendence of earthly desires.

Legacy

- **Influence**: Akka Mahadevi is considered one of the early proponents of the Bhakti movement in South India. Her works have inspired many generations of poets and spiritual seekers, highlighting the transformative power of devotion and personal spiritual experience.

- **Recognition**: She is revered as a saint and poet, and her life and works are celebrated in various literary and cultural contexts. Her legacy continues to influence contemporary spiritual and literary thought, making her an enduring figure in the annals of Indian spirituality and literature.

Channabasavanna was a prominent 12th-century Kannada poet and philosopher, esteemed for his significant contributions to the Lingayat tradition. His life and works have left an indelible mark on the spiritual and cultural heritage of the Lingayat community. Here are detailed aspects of his life and contributions:

Literary Contributions

"Viveka Chintamani"

- Renowned Work: Channabasavanna's most renowned work is the "Viveka Chintamani," a seminal text in the Veerashaiva tradition. This literary masterpiece delves into the essence of personal spiritual experience and underscores the importance of unwavering devotion to Lord Shiva. The text serves as a guide for devotees seeking a deeper understanding of their spiritual path.
- Content and Themes: "Viveka Chintamani" explores various facets of spirituality, devotion, and ethical living. It provides insights into the nature of the self, the divine, and the path to spiritual enlightenment. The text emphasizes the significance of introspection, self-discipline, and sincere devotion in one's spiritual journey.

Philosophical Insights

Emphasis on Devotion

- Significance of Personal Experience: Channabasavanna's writings emphasize the importance of personal spiritual experiences and a direct connection with the divine. He believed that true devotion to Lord Shiva transcends ritualistic practices and is rooted in heartfelt worship and ethical living.
- Heartfelt Worship: His philosophical insights advocate for a sincere and personal approach to spirituality. Channabasavanna's teachings encourage devotees to cultivate a deep, personal relationship with the divine through love, devotion, and moral integrity.
- Critique of Ritualism: Channabasavanna critiqued the overemphasis on rituals and external ceremonies, arguing that true spirituality lies in inner transformation and the cultivation of virtues. His teachings urge individuals to focus on the essence of devotion rather than the form.

Spiritual Legacy

- Enduring Influence: Through his profound philosophical insights and poetic expressions, Channabasavanna has left an enduring legacy that continues to inspire spiritual seekers and scholars in the Lingayat community. His works remain a source of inspiration and guidance for those on the spiritual path.
- Contribution to Lingayat Thought: His contributions have enriched the philosophical and literary tradition of Lingayatism, providing a deeper understanding of the principles of devotion, equality, and ethical living. Channabasavanna's writings have played a crucial role in shaping the spiritual and cultural ethos of the Lingayat community.

Nephew of Basavanna

- Influential Relationship: Channabasavanna was indeed the nephew of Basavanna, a revered philosopher and statesman who played a pivotal role in the Bhakti movement in Karnataka. Their familial and spiritual bond significantly influenced Channabasavanna's own spiritual journey and contributions.
- Shared Vision: The relationship between Channabasavanna and Basavanna was marked by a shared vision of spiritual reform and social justice. Basavanna's teachings and leadership deeply impacted Channabasavanna, inspiring him to continue the work of promoting devotion to Lord Shiva and advocating for social equality.
- Collaborative Efforts: Together, they contributed to the spread and consolidation of the Lingayat movement, emphasizing the values of devotion, ethical living, and social inclusivity. Their collaborative efforts have left a lasting impact on the spiritual and cultural landscape of Karnataka.

Channabasavanna's life and works have made significant contributions to the Veerashaiva tradition. His literary masterpiece, "Viveka Chintamani," along with his profound philosophical insights, continue to inspire and guide devotees. As the nephew of Basavanna, Channabasavanna's spiritual journey was deeply influenced by their familial bond, resulting in a shared vision of devotion and social reform. His enduring legacy reflects the core principles of Lingayatism, including unwavering devotion to Lord Shiva, the importance of personal spiritual experiences, and a commitment to ethical living. Channabasavanna's disciples, such as Siddharameshwar and Lakshmidevi, along with Akkamahadevi, have made significant contributions to the spiritual and cultural heritage of Lingayatism. Their Vachanas and exemplary lives reflect the core principles of devotion, equality, and ethical living that are central to the faith. Their legacies continue to inspire and guide devotees, emphasizing the enduring relevance of their teachings and the importance of inclusivity and spiritual integrity in the Lingayat tradition

CHAPTER THIRTEEN

Allam Prabhu: A Luminary of Lingayatism

Early Life
Birth and Family

- Birth: Allam Prabhu was born in the early 12th century in Balligavi, a historic town in the Shimoga district of Karnataka. While his exact birth date remains undocumented, his life and legacy are deeply etched in the spiritual and cultural history of the region. Balligavi, known for its rich cultural heritage, provided a fertile ground for his spiritual journey.

- Parents: Allam Prabhu was born to Nirashankara and Sujnani, who were devout followers of the Shaiva tradition. Their spiritual inclinations significantly influenced Allam Prabhu's early life, fostering a deep devotion to Lord Shiva from a young age. His upbringing in a spiritually enriched environment laid the foundation for his future contributions to the Lingayat movement.

Contributions
Vachana Poetry
Renowned Poet

- Vachana Poetry: Allam Prabhu is celebrated for his Vachana poetry, a form of brief, pithy poetic prose written in Kannada. These Vachanas are characterized by their profound spiritual insights and lyrical beauty. His poetry addresses various aspects of spirituality, devotion, and social issues, making it a cornerstone of Lingayat literature.
- Unity of Self and Shiva: His Vachanas emphasize the unity of the self (Atman) and Shiva (Paramatman), advocating for a direct and personal experience of the divine. Through his poetry, Allam Prabhu critiqued the ritualistic practices and social conventions of the time, encouraging a more personal and heartfelt approach to spirituality. His Vachanas invite readers to transcend external rituals and connect with the divine on a deeper, more personal level.

Advaita and Monotheism
Message of Non-Dualism

- Advaita (Non-Dualism): Allam Prabhu's verses spread the message of Advaita, promoting the idea that there is only one ultimate reality, which is Shiva. His teachings encourage single-minded devotion to Lord Shiva, transcending the boundaries of traditional religious practices. This non-dualistic philosophy emphasizes the inherent oneness of all existence.
- Spiritual Teachings: His poetry and teachings advocate for a spiritual journey centered on inner realization and

the dissolution of the ego. Allam Prabhu believed that true enlightenment comes from understanding the oneness of all existence. His teachings inspire devotees to seek the divine within themselves and recognize the interconnectedness of all life.

Social Reform
Breaking Social Barriers

- Tool for Social Reform: Allam Prabhu used his poetry as a powerful tool for social reform, breaking down the barriers of caste, class, and religious orthodoxy. His Vachanas emphasize moral values, equality, and devotional worship, challenging the societal norms that perpetuated discrimination and inequality. His writings call for a more just and inclusive society, where all individuals are valued and respected.
- Champion of Equality: He was a strong proponent of social justice, advocating for a society where all individuals are valued and respected, regardless of their social status or background. His efforts to promote equality and challenge social hierarchies have left a lasting impact on the Lingayat community and beyond.

Legacy
Anubhava Mantapa
Key Figure

- Anubhava Mantapa: Allam Prabhu was a key figure in the Anubhava Mantapa, the spiritual and philosophical forum established by Basavanna. The Anubhava Mantapa served as a hub for intellectual and spiritual discussions, promoting the principles of Lingayatism.

This inclusive forum welcomed individuals from diverse backgrounds to share their spiritual insights and engage in meaningful dialogue.

- Presiding Guru: He is often considered the real guru who presided over the Anubhava Mantapa, guiding the debates and discussions with his profound wisdom and spiritual insights. His role in the Anubhava Mantapa was pivotal in shaping the spiritual and philosophical discourse of the time.

Trinity of Lingayatism
Celebrated Saint

- Trinity of Lingayatism: Along with Basavanna and Akka Mahadevi, Allam Prabhu is celebrated as one of the "Trinity of Lingayatism." This trinity is revered for its contributions to the spiritual, literary, and social fabric of the Lingayat community. Together, they have left an indelible mark on the tradition, inspiring countless generations of devotees.
- Enduring Influence: His teachings and poetry continue to inspire spiritual seekers and promote the values of equality, devotion, and social reform. The enduring relevance of his contributions reflects the timeless wisdom and spiritual depth of his teachings.

Philosophical Influence

Allam Prabhu's philosophy is rooted in the principles of non-dualism and monotheism. His teachings advocate for a deep, personal connection with the divine, transcending ritualistic practices and societal norms. His emphasis on inner realization and the unity of self and Shiva encourages devotees to seek spiritual enlightenment through personal experience and self-reflection. His Vachanas serve as a guide for those on the spiritual path, offering insights into the nature of existence and the journey towards self-realization.

Nagamma

- **Early Life**: Nagamma was a devoted follower of Allamaprabhu, one of the prominent saints of Lingayatism. She was known for her deep spiritual insights and unwavering devotion. Her life was marked by a profound dedication to spiritual practice and a deep connection to the teachings of Allamaprabhu.
- **Contributions**: Nagamma's Vachanas (devotional poems) reflect her profound spiritual experiences and her commitment to the principles of Lingayatism. Her works are celebrated for their philosophical depth and lyrical beauty. Her writings continue to inspire devotees and scholars alike, highlighting the enduring relevance of her spiritual insights.

Muktayakka

- **Spiritual Journey**: Muktayakka was another significant female disciple of Allamaprabhu. She was known for her intense spiritual practices and her dedication to the path of self-realization. Her life was marked by a relentless pursuit of spiritual truth and a deep commitment to personal transformation.
- **Literary Contributions**: Muktayakka's Vachanas are revered for their spiritual wisdom and their emphasis on the importance of personal devotion and ethical living. Her writings continue to inspire devotees and scholars alike, showcasing her profound spiritual insights and her

dedication to the principles of Lingayatism.

Sharane Sri Danamma Devi and the female disciples of Allamaprabhu like Nagamma and Muktayakka exemplify the profound contributions of women in Lingayatism. Their lives and works reflect the core principles of devotion, service, and equality that are central to the faith. Through their spiritual insights, community service, and unwavering commitment to ethical living, they have left an indelible mark on the Lingayat tradition and continue to inspire generations of devotees.Allam Prabhu's life and contributions to Lingayatism have left an indelible mark on the spiritual and cultural heritage of the community. His profound Vachana poetry, teachings on non-dualism, and efforts in social reform continue to inspire and guide devotees. As a key figure in the Anubhava Mantapa and a celebrated member of the "Trinity of Lingayatism," his legacy endures, promoting the values of equality, devotion, and inner realization.

Social & Economic Impact

- *The Significance and Socio-Economic Impact of Dasoha*

- *Lingayats and Their Strong Tradition of Valuing Education*

- *Kayaka: The Concept of Work as Worship in Lingayatism*

- *The Ishtalinga Initiation and Gender Equality in Lingayatism*

- *Anubhava Mantapa: A Revolutionary Forum Promoting Gender Equality and Inclusivity*

The Significance and Socio-Economic Impact of Dasoha

Dasoha is a fundamental principle in Lingayatism that emphasizes the importance of **service to others**. The term is derived from the Sanskrit words "das," meaning "servant," and "oha," meaning "giving." It reflects the spirit of compassion, generosity, and community service. Let's delve deeper into its significance and socio-economic impact:

Significance of Dasoha

Core Principles

- **Service to Society**: Dasoha involves selflessly serving others, providing food, shelter, and support to those in need. This principle reflects the teachings of Basavanna, who emphasized that service to humanity is a form of worship.
- **Community Support**: Dasoha encourages individuals to dedicate a part of their time, effort, and income to support the community and religious mendicants

(Jangama). This practice fosters a sense of solidarity and mutual aid within the community.

- **Spiritual Significance**: In Lingayatism, Dasoha is considered a means to attain spiritual growth and salvation. By serving others selflessly, individuals can purify their hearts and minds, drawing closer to the divine.

Practical Implementation of Dasoha
Anna Dasoha

- **Providing Food**: One of the most common forms of Dasoha is Anna Dasoha, which involves providing food to the hungry. This practice is especially significant in schools, where many Lingayat communities run programs to supply midday meals to students. For example, the famous Mathas and Foundation Foundation, supported by many Lingayat donors, provides nutritious meals to millions of children across India.

- **Community Kitchens**: Many Lingayat temples and institutions operate community kitchens that offer free meals to all, regardless of their social or economic status. These kitchens serve as a practical demonstration of the principle of selfless service.

Charitable Activities

- **Supporting Education**: Lingayat communities are actively involved in supporting educational institutions, providing scholarships, and facilitating access to education for underprivileged children. By investing in education, they contribute to the long-term socio-economic development of society.

- **Health and Welfare**: Engaging in various charitable acts, such as donating to the needy, supporting healthcare initiatives, and participating in community service projects, Lingayats address immediate needs and promote overall well-being.

Historical Context
12th Century Sharana Movement

- **Advocacy by Saints**: The concept of Dasoha was strongly advocated by the Sharana movement, led by Basavanna and other saints. They emphasized social equality and community welfare, challenging the rigid caste system and promoting the idea that service to humanity is a path to divine realization.
- **Revolutionary Impact**: This movement was revolutionary for its time, as it sought to create a more just and inclusive society by encouraging individuals to engage in selfless service and support one another.

Socio-Economic Impact
Social Impact

- **Promoting Equality**: Dasoha promotes social equality by encouraging individuals to serve others without discrimination. It helps bridge social divides and fosters a sense of unity and inclusivity within the community.
- **Empowerment of Marginalized Groups**: By providing food, education, and healthcare, Dasoha initiatives empower marginalized groups, giving them the tools and support they need to improve their quality of life.

Economic Impact

- **Alleviating Poverty**: By addressing immediate needs such as hunger and lack of education, Dasoha initiatives help alleviate poverty and create opportunities for socio-economic advancement. For example, providing midday meals in schools improves children's attendance and academic performance, setting the stage for a brighter future.
- **Sustainable Development**: Investing in education, healthcare, and community welfare contributes to sustainable development. Dasoha initiatives create a more resilient and self-sufficient society by equipping individuals with the skills and resources they need to thrive.

Cultural and Historical Significance
Sharana Movement

- **Historical Roots**: Dasoha is deeply rooted in the 12th-century Sharana movement, a significant socio-religious reform led by Basavanna and other saints. This movement aimed to create an egalitarian society by challenging the rigid caste system and promoting social justice.
- **Revolutionary Impact**: The Sharana movement was revolutionary for its time, advocating for equality and inclusivity. Dasoha, as a practice, was integral to this movement, embodying the principles of selfless service and community support. For instance, the Anubhava Mantapa, established by Basavanna, was a hub for discussing social issues and implementing practices like Dasoha to address societal needs.

Cultural Integration

- **Embedded in Tradition**: Dasoha is embedded in the cultural fabric of Lingayat communities, influencing their social norms and practices. It has become a way of life, shaping how Lingayats interact with each other and the broader society. For example, during festivals and community events, Lingayats organize community feasts and charitable activities, reflecting the spirit of Dasoha.

- **Generational Practice**: The practice of Dasoha is passed down through generations, ensuring that the values of compassion, generosity, and service remain central to the community's identity. Stories of saints and their selfless deeds are shared within families and community gatherings, inspiring younger generations to carry forward the tradition.

Egalitarian Philosophy
Rejecting Caste and Class

- **True Equality**: Unlike some other traditions where charity might still be influenced by social hierarchies, Dasoha explicitly rejects caste and class distinctions, promoting true equality in service. This means that when performing acts of Dasoha, Lingayats serve everyone equally, regardless of their social status. For instance, community kitchens and food distribution programs are open to all, reflecting the principle of non-discrimination.

- **Universal Participation**: Dasoha encourages every individual to participate in service, regardless of their social standing. This inclusive approach reinforces the community's commitment to social justice and equality. By engaging in Dasoha, individuals from different backgrounds come together, fostering a sense of unity and mutual respect.

Empowerment

- **Empowering Service**: Dasoha empowers every individual to contribute to the well-being of their community. It instills a sense of purpose and responsibility, allowing people to take active roles in supporting others. For example, individuals might organize educational programs, provide medical assistance, or engage in environmental conservation efforts as part of their Dasoha activities.
- **Reinforcing Social Justice**: Through the practice of Dasoha, Lingayats actively promote social justice and equality. It serves as a practical expression of their commitment to creating a fair and just society. By participating in charitable acts and community service, Lingayats work towards uplifting the marginalized and addressing social inequalities.

Dasoha is a beautiful practice that embodies the spirit of compassion, generosity, and community service. Its significance lies in its ability to promote social equality, spiritual growth, and socio-economic development. Through various forms of selfless service, Lingayats continue to make a positive impact on society, upholding the teachings of Basavanna and fostering a more just and inclusive world.These unique aspects make Dasoha a distinctive and integral part of Lingayatism, reflecting the core values of the tradition and its emphasis on practical, community-oriented spirituality. By embracing Dasoha, Lingayats not only honor the teachings of Basavanna but also contribute to the betterment of society, fostering a culture of compassion, equality, and selfless service.

CHAPTER FIFTEEN

Lingayats and Their Strong Tradition of Valuing Education

Lingayats have a rich tradition of valuing education, deeply intertwined with their socio-religious practices. From the 12th century to the present day, they have established numerous educational institutions aimed at promoting learning, equality, and social upliftment. Let's elaborate on their involvement in education with specific examples:

Historical Context

1. 12th Century Foundations

- **Social Reform**: The foundation of Lingayatism by Basavanna in the 12th century marked a period of significant social reform. Basavanna emphasized education as a means to achieve social equality and justice. His teachings encouraged learning and critical thinking, laying the groundwork for a tradition that highly values education.

- ○ **Example**: Basavanna's emphasis on education can be seen in his establishment of the Anubhava Mantapa, a center for learning and dialogue, where individuals from all backgrounds could discuss spiritual and social issues.

- **Sharana Movement**: The Sharana movement, led by Basavanna and other saints, promoted literacy and education as powerful tools for social change and empowerment. This movement sought to challenge the prevailing social order and create a more egalitarian society through education and awareness.

  - ○ **Example**: The Vachanas written by Basavanna and other Sharanas are not only spiritual texts but also contain social critiques and calls for reform, advocating for the spread of literacy and education to combat social inequalities.

Educational Institutions
1. Mathas (Monasteries)

- **Centers of Learning**: Historically, Lingayat mathas (monasteries) have served as important centers of learning. These institutions offered both religious and secular education, fostering an environment where knowledge and spiritual growth went hand in hand. Mathas played a crucial role in promoting the teachings of Basavanna and other Lingayat saints.

  - ○ **Example**: The Siddaganga Matha in Tumkur, Karnataka, is renowned for its contributions to education. It runs numerous schools and colleges, offering free education to thousands of students, including those from marginalized communities.

- **Shaiva Studies**: Mathas have been pivotal in promoting Shaiva studies, ensuring that the teachings and philosophy of Lingayatism are preserved and propagated. They provided a structured environment for studying religious texts, philosophy, and ethics.

  - **Example**: The Murugha Matha in Chitradurga, Karnataka, has been a center for Shaiva studies, offering courses in Lingayat philosophy and religious practices. It also supports various educational initiatives for the broader community.

2. Modern Schools and Colleges

- **Expansion of Educational Institutions**: In modern times, many Lingayat communities have established schools, colleges, and universities to provide quality education to their members and the broader community. These institutions uphold the tradition of valuing education and aim to make learning accessible to all.

  - **Example**: The Basaveshwara Medical College in Chitradurga and the Basaveshwara Engineering College in Bagalkot are prominent institutions established by the Lingayat community, providing quality education in medical and engineering fields.

- **Focus on Secular Education**: While maintaining their religious teachings, Lingayat educational institutions also focus on secular subjects, ensuring a well-rounded education for students. This approach prepares students for various professional fields and contributes to overall societal development.

- ○ **Example**: The S. Nijalingappa College in Bengaluru offers a wide range of secular courses alongside its religious and cultural education programs, ensuring that students receive a comprehensive education.

Focus on Social Justice
1. Inclusive Education

- **Opportunities for All**: Lingayat institutions emphasize inclusive education, providing opportunities for students from all backgrounds, including marginalized communities. By ensuring that education is accessible to everyone, these institutions promote social justice and equality.

  - ○ **Example**: The Siddaganga Education Society runs over 125 educational institutions, offering education from primary to postgraduate levels, with a focus on inclusivity and support for economically disadvantaged students.

- **Community Support**: Various programs and initiatives support students from disadvantaged backgrounds, helping them overcome barriers to education and achieve their full potential.

  - ○ **Example**: The midday meal scheme (Anna Dasoha) implemented by many Lingayat schools ensures that students receive nutritious meals, improving attendance and academic performance.

2. Scholarships and Support

- **Financial Assistance**: Numerous scholarships and support programs are available to encourage students to pursue higher education and professional careers. These initiatives help reduce financial burdens and make higher education more accessible.

  - **Example**: The Karnataka Lingayat Education Society offers various scholarships for meritorious and financially needy students, promoting higher education among the Lingayat community.

- **Mentorship and Guidance**: Lingayat institutions often provide mentorship and guidance to students, helping them navigate their educational journeys and achieve their goals.

  - **Example**: Mentorship programs in institutions like the Lingayat Educational Association provide students with the guidance and support needed to excel in their studies and careers.

Contemporary Impact
1. Promotion of Literacy

- **Educational Outreach**: Lingayat organizations continue to promote literacy and education as essential components of social development and empowerment. Initiatives like literacy drives, adult education programs, and community learning centers contribute to this mission.

- ○ **Example**: The Lingayat Education Society's adult education programs help improve literacy rates among adults in rural areas, empowering them with basic reading and writing skills.

- **Anna Dasoha Programs**: Programs like midday meal schemes (Anna Dasoha) in schools ensure that students receive nutritious meals, which improves attendance and academic performance, further promoting literacy and education.

- ○ **Example**: The midday meal program at the Siddaganga Matha has been instrumental in improving school attendance and nutritional standards among children.

2. Community Engagement

- **Holistic Development**: Education is seen as a means to uplift the community and address social issues. Lingayat institutions align with the core principles of Dasoha (selfless service) and community support, emphasizing holistic development.

- ○ **Example**: Community health initiatives, environmental awareness programs, and vocational training are part of the holistic education approach at many Lingayat institutions.

- **Empowerment Through Education**: By providing quality education and fostering a culture of lifelong learning, Lingayat institutions empower individuals to contribute positively to society and drive social change.

  - **Example**: The alumni of Lingayat educational institutions often engage in community service, social entrepreneurship, and advocacy for social justice, reflecting the values instilled during their education.

Educational Institutions

- **BLDE University**: Established in 2008, BLDE University offers a variety of undergraduate, postgraduate, and doctoral programs in fields such as medicine, engineering, pharmacy, and more. The university is committed to providing high-quality education and fostering research and innovation.
- **Shri B.M. Patil Medical College**: Known for its excellence in medical education, this college offers programs including MBBS, postgraduate, and super-specialty courses. It is renowned for its state-of-the-art facilities and experienced faculty.
- **Engineering and Technology Colleges**: BLDEA runs several engineering colleges, including the V.P. Dr. P.G. Halakatti College of Engineering & Technology. These institutions offer diverse engineering programs aimed at producing skilled professionals in various technical fields.
- **Allied Health Sciences**: The association also offers programs in physiotherapy, nursing, and other allied health sciences, ensuring comprehensive healthcare

education and training.

Achievements

- **Rankings**: BLDEA's institutions have received recognition for their quality education. For instance, the V.P. Dr. P.G. Halakatti College of Engineering & Technology was ranked 53rd in the All India Ranking by the Times Survey 2020, reflecting its academic excellence.
- **Global Collaboration**: The association collaborates with universities worldwide, providing a global perspective to its curriculum. These partnerships enhance educational quality and offer students exposure to international academic standards.

Historical Significance

- **Founding Vision**: Founded by Dr. P.G. Halakatti, a social reformer and literary figure, BLDEA has a rich history of over 100 years. Dr. Halakatti's vision of education as a means for social reform continues to guide the association's activities.
- **Leadership**: Visionary leaders like Shri B.M. Patil and Shri M.B. Patil have been instrumental in expanding and diversifying the association's activities. Their leadership has ensured that BLDEA remains a significant contributor to the region's educational and social development.

KLE Society and Its Contributions to Education

The KLE Society, founded in 1916 by a group of dedicated teachers known as the "Saptarishis" or "Seven

Saints," has been a beacon of quality education in India for nearly a century. The founding members included Prof. M.R. Sakhaare, Prof. S.S. Basavanal, Shri. B.B. Mamdapur, Dr. H.F. Kattimani, Prof. B.S. Hanchinal, Prof. P.R. Chikodi, and Prof. P.R. Chikodi. Their vision and commitment to education have led to the establishment of over 270 institutions across Karnataka and Maharashtra, offering educational services from pre-primary to post-doctoral studies3.

Dasoha, a revered concept rooted in the philosophy of selfless service and compassion, is integral to the Veerashaiva tradition. It embodies the act of giving generously and willingly, without any expectation of personal gain2. In the context of KLE Society, Dasoha extends beyond material offerings to include sharing knowledge, time, and positive energy. This principle of selfless service fosters a sense of unity and interconnectedness among individuals, creating a harmonious environment where the act of giving is considered a noble and spiritually enriching endeavor

Sharanabasappa Appa Kalburgi, the esteemed pontiff of the Sharana Basaveshwara Samsthana in Kalaburagi, has made significant contributions to education in the region. Under his leadership, the Sharana Basaveshwara Samsthana has established a chain of educational institutions that provide quality education to students from various backgrounds1. His vision has been instrumental in promoting literacy and empowering the youth through access to education.

In addition to his educational initiatives, Sharanabasappa Appa Kalburgi has been a strong advocate for the principles of Dasoha (selfless service) and Kayaka (righteous work). These principles have been integrated into the curriculum of the institutions, fostering a culture of giving and ethical living among students. His efforts have not only enhanced the educational landscape but also instilled values of compassion and social responsibility in the younger generation.

Dr. Sampatkumar S. Shivanagi, a prominent Lingayat and visionary philanthropist based in the USA, has made a remarkable contribution to the KLE Society by funding the establishment of the KLE Dr. Sampatkumar S. Shivanagi Cancer Hospital in Belagavi. This state-of-the-art facility, inaugurated by President Droupadi Murmu on December 30, 2024, is equipped with cutting-edge technology and offers comprehensive cancer care services under one roof1. The hospital, spread over 1,75,000 square feet, includes advanced treatment options such as bone marrow transplants, robotic surgery, and genomic-guided precision care.

Dr. Shivanagi's generous donation of ₹8 crores has enabled the hospital to provide subsidized treatment through various government schemes, ensuring that quality healthcare is accessible to all. His philanthropic efforts reflect a deep commitment to improving healthcare infrastructure and supporting the community in North Karnataka1. The KLE Dr. Sampatkumar S. Shivanagi Cancer Hospital stands as a testament to his dedication to the well-being of others and his vision for a healthier future.

The Lingayat community's strong tradition of valuing education has made significant contributions to social upliftment and empowerment. From historical mathas to modern educational institutions, the focus on inclusive and quality education continues to promote social justice and holistic development. Lingayat institutions remain dedicated to fostering a culture of learning, inclusivity, and service, ensuring that Basavanna's legacy lives on through their efforts.

CHAPTER SIXTEEN

Kayaka: The Concept of Work as Worship in Lingayatism

Kayaka: Work as Worship in Lingayatism

Kayaka is a fundamental concept in Lingayatism, emphasizing the importance of work and labor as a form of worship. This principle integrates spirituality with everyday work, promoting a balanced and fulfilling life. Here is a detailed exploration of Kayaka and its significance:

Meaning and Significance

Work as Worship

- **Definition**: Kayaka translates to "work" or "labor," signifying that all forms of work, when performed with dedication and sincerity, are considered a form of worship. It transforms mundane tasks into spiritual acts, infusing daily activities with a sense of purpose and devotion.

- **Spiritual Growth**: Engaging in Kayaka allows individuals to attain spiritual growth and liberation. It is believed that salvation comes through devotion to one's occupation, as work is seen as an expression of one's commitment to the divine.

Principles of Kayaka
Equality in Work

- **Valuing All Work**: Kayaka promotes the idea that all work, regardless of its nature, is valuable and should be performed with equal dedication. This principle challenges the hierarchical division of labor, emphasizing that every job, whether manual or intellectual, has inherent dignity and worth.
- **Breaking Down Barriers**: By valuing all forms of work equally, Kayaka helps break down social barriers and promotes a more inclusive and egalitarian society.

Dedication and Effort

- **Sincere Effort**: Kayaka emphasizes the importance of putting in sincere effort and dedication into one's work. This approach honors the divine by transforming daily tasks into acts of devotion, encouraging individuals to strive for excellence and integrity in their professions.
- **Holistic Approach**: It encourages a holistic approach to life, where work is not seen as separate from spiritual practice but as an integral part of one's spiritual journey.

Historical Context
Basavanna's Teachings

- **Advocacy of Kayaka**: The concept of Kayaka was strongly advocated by Basavanna, the founder of

Lingayatism. He believed that work is a means to achieve spiritual liberation and that devotion to one's occupation can lead to salvation. Basavanna's teachings emphasized that true spirituality is found in the fulfillment of one's duties with sincerity and dedication.

Social Reform

- **Promoting Equality**: Kayaka was also a part of Basavanna's broader social reform agenda. By promoting equality and rejecting the caste-based division of labor, Basavanna sought to create a more just and inclusive society. The principle of Kayaka challenged the traditional social hierarchy, advocating for the dignity of labor and the equality of all individuals.

Modern Practice
Community Service

- **Aligning with Dasoha**: In contemporary Lingayat communities, Kayaka continues to be practiced through various forms of community service and social work. These activities align with the principles of Dasoha (service to others) and embody the spirit of selfless service and dedication.
- **Practical Implementation**: Examples include organizing community events, participating in social welfare programs, and contributing to the betterment of society through volunteer work.

Educational Institutions

- **Incorporating Kayaka**: Many Lingayat educational institutions incorporate the concept of Kayaka in their curriculum. They encourage students to engage in meaningful work and community service, fostering a sense of responsibility and dedication from a young age.
- **Holistic Education**: By integrating Kayaka into their teaching methods, these institutions promote holistic education that values both academic excellence and ethical living.

Examples and Implementation

1. **Historical Context and Basavanna's Teachings**

   ◦ **Example**: Basavanna's own life exemplified the principle of Kayaka. As a statesman and a spiritual leader, he performed his duties with utmost dedication and integrity, demonstrating that work and worship are not separate but intertwined.

2. **Modern Practice in Community Service**

   ◦ **Example**: The Siddaganga Matha in Tumkur, Karnataka, embodies the principle of Kayaka through its numerous social welfare activities. The Matha provides free education, food, and shelter to thousands of students and pilgrims, reflecting the spirit of selfless service and dedication.

3. **Educational Institutions Incorporating Kayaka**

   ◦ **Example**: The Basaveshwara Engineering College in Bagalkot encourages students to engage in community service projects as part of their curriculum. These projects not only benefit the community but also instill a sense of responsibility and ethical living in the students.

Kayaka is a significant concept in Lingayatism that emphasizes the importance of work and labor as a form of worship. By integrating spirituality with everyday work, Kayaka promotes a balanced and fulfilling life. Through its principles of equality, dedication, and holistic approach, Kayaka continues to inspire individuals and institutions to strive for excellence and integrity in their professions and community service. Basavanna's teachings and the modern practice of Kayaka highlight its enduring relevance and transformative impact on society.

The Ishtalinga Initiation and Gender Equality in Lingayatism

The Ishtalinga Initiation, also known as Ishtalinga Deeksha, is a significant practice in Lingayatism that stands out for promoting gender equality. Here's an elaboration on this aspect:

Universal Accessibility
Inclusivity

- **Open to All:** The Ishtalinga initiation ceremony is inclusive and open to all individuals, regardless of their gender, social status, or caste. This inclusivity reflects the fundamental Lingayat principle of equality, where everyone has the right to spiritual practices and the opportunity to connect with the divine. The ceremony emphasizes that spirituality and devotion are accessible to everyone, breaking down traditional barriers that have historically excluded certain groups.
- **Equal Participation:** Both men and women participate equally in the rituals and are equally entitled to receive

the Ishtalinga Deeksha. There is no discrimination based on gender, ensuring that everyone can embark on their spiritual journey on an equal footing. This practice highlights the Lingayat commitment to gender equality and the belief that both men and women have equal spiritual potential and responsibilities.

Symbol of Equality
Ishtalinga

- **Personal Symbol of Devotion**: The Ishtalinga worn by every initiate serves as a personal symbol of their devotion to Lord Shiva. This practice underscores the belief that spiritual devotion transcends gender boundaries. The Ishtalinga is a constant reminder of one's commitment to the divine, fostering a sense of spiritual equality. By wearing the Ishtalinga, individuals affirm their personal relationship with Shiva, irrespective of their gender or social status.
- **Direct Connection to the Divine**: The Ishtalinga provides a direct and personal connection to the divine, emphasizing that spiritual growth and enlightenment are accessible to all, regardless of gender. This direct connection eliminates the need for intermediaries, reinforcing the idea of personal spirituality. It empowers individuals to take charge of their spiritual journey and experience the divine presence directly in their lives.

Historical Context
Basavanna's Teachings

- **Advocacy for Gender Equality**: Basavanna, the founder of Lingayatism, and the Sharana movement strongly advocated for gender equality. They challenged traditional norms that discriminated against women and promoted the idea that both men and women have equal rights to spiritual knowledge and practices. Basavanna's teachings consistently emphasized the inherent worth and dignity of every individual, regardless of gender, and sought to create a more just and inclusive society.

- **Rejection of Discrimination**: Basavanna's rebellion against the exclusion of his sister from the thread ceremony is a notable example of his commitment to gender equality. He protested against rituals that marginalized women and worked towards ensuring that everyone, regardless of gender, had equal access to spiritual practices.

Women's Role
Active Participation

- **Active Participation**: Historical texts and Vachanas (devotional poems) from female Sharanas (saints) like Akka Mahadevi highlight the active participation of women in spiritual and social discourse. These texts reflect the significant contributions of women to the spiritual and cultural heritage of Lingayatism. Female saints played a vital role in shaping the movement, demonstrating their intellectual and spiritual prowess.

- **Empowerment Through Literature**: The writings of female saints emphasize themes of devotion, spiritual longing, and social justice, showcasing the empowered role of women in the Lingayat tradition. Their Vachanas often address issues of gender equality and advocate for the rights and dignity of women in spiritual and social spheres.

The Ishtalinga Initiation, or Ishtalinga Deeksha, is a powerful practice in Lingayatism that promotes gender equality and inclusivity. By ensuring universal accessibility and equal participation in spiritual practices, it reinforces the Lingayat principles of equality and personal devotion. Basavanna's teachings and the active role of women in the Lingayat tradition further highlight the commitment to gender equality and the empowerment of all individuals in their spiritual journey. The Ishtalinga serves as a personal symbol of devotion and a reminder that spiritual growth and enlightenment are accessible to everyone, regardless of gender or social status.

CHAPTER EIGHTEEN

Anubhava Mantapa: A Revolutionary Forum Promoting Gender Equality and Inclusivity

The Anubhava Mantapa, established by Basavanna in the 12th century, was a groundbreaking institution that played a crucial role in advancing gender equality and inclusivity. Here are the detailed aspects of its contributions:

Inclusive Participation

Open to All

- **Welcoming All Individuals**: The Anubhava Mantapa was open to individuals from all walks of life, regardless of their gender, social status, or caste. This inclusivity was revolutionary at the time, as it provided a platform for open and egalitarian discourse. Women, who were often excluded from religious and philosophical debates, were given equal opportunities to participate and share their insights.

- **Example**: The participation of diverse individuals in the Anubhava Mantapa highlighted its commitment to inclusivity. This platform allowed voices from different backgrounds to be heard and respected, fostering a culture of mutual respect and understanding.

Breaking Social Norms

- **Challenging Hierarchies**: The Anubhava Mantapa challenged the rigid social hierarchies and religious orthodoxy of the time. It served as a forum where marginalized voices, including those of women, could be heard and respected. This was a significant departure from the prevalent norms that restricted women's participation in religious and intellectual activities.

  - **Example**: The Anubhava Mantapa's inclusive approach empowered marginalized groups, enabling them to contribute to religious and philosophical discussions on equal footing with others.

Key Female Figures
Akka Mahadevi

- **Prominent Female Participant**: Akka Mahadevi, one of the most prominent female figures in the Lingayat tradition, actively participated in the Anubhava Mantapa. Her debates and spiritual insights were highly respected, and she became renowned for her profound spiritual convictions. Akka Mahadevi's participation challenged patriarchal norms and demonstrated that women could hold significant spiritual and intellectual authority.

- ○ **Example**: Akka Mahadevi's Vachanas (devotional poems) are celebrated for their deep philosophical and spiritual content, addressing themes of divine love, personal devotion, and social justice.

Other Female Sharanas

- **Diverse Contributions**: Several other female saints and poets, known as Sharanas, also contributed to the rich tapestry of intellectual and spiritual discourse at the Anubhava Mantapa. These women played vital roles in shaping the spiritual and cultural ethos of the Lingayat community.

  - ○ **Example**: The contributions of female Sharanas like Akka Nagamma and Akka Mahadevi were embraced and valued, highlighting the inclusive nature of the Anubhava Mantapa and their significant influence on Lingayat literature and philosophy.

Spiritual and Social Equality
Equal Recognition

- **Valuing Women's Contributions**: Women's contributions to religious experience were not only accepted but were also significantly valued and celebrated. The Anubhava Mantapa recognized the spiritual insights and intellectual capabilities of women, providing them with a platform to express and develop their spiritual thoughts.

- ◦ **Example**: The inclusion and celebration of women's contributions in the Anubhava Mantapa set a precedent for recognizing and valuing gender equality in spiritual and intellectual realms.

Spiritual Leadership

- **Positions of Leadership**: Female participants held positions of spiritual leadership and were recognized for their spiritual stature and contributions. Their leadership roles in the Anubhava Mantapa demonstrated that gender was not a barrier to achieving spiritual prominence and respect.

  - ◦ **Example**: Women like Akka Mahadevi held respected positions of spiritual leadership, and their teachings continue to inspire the Lingayat community, reflecting the enduring impact of their contributions.

Legacy
Inspiration for Modern Movements

- **Continuing Influence**: The principles of gender equality and inclusivity promoted by the Anubhava Mantapa continue to inspire modern movements and social reforms. The forum's progressive vision remains relevant, encouraging contemporary efforts to achieve gender equality and social justice.

  - ◦ **Example**: Contemporary movements advocating for gender equality and social justice often draw inspiration from the inclusive principles of the

Anubhava Mantapa, highlighting its lasting impact on modern social reforms.

- **Model for Inclusivity**: The Anubhava Mantapa serves as a model for inclusive and egalitarian practices in various spheres of life, including religious, social, and educational contexts.

  - **Example**: Organizations and institutions that promote inclusivity and equality often look to the Anubhava Mantapa as a model for creating environments where diverse voices are heard and respected.

Educational Impact

- **Influence on Institutions**: The legacy of gender equality in the Anubhava Mantapa has significantly influenced contemporary educational institutions and community practices within the Lingayat community. These institutions continue to uphold the values of inclusivity and equality, providing equal opportunities for education and leadership to both men and women.

  - **Example**: Educational institutions like the Basaveshwara Educational Society promote inclusive education, ensuring that both men and women have equal opportunities for academic and personal growth.

- **Promotion of Egalitarian Values**: By promoting egalitarian values, the Anubhava Mantapa has left an enduring impact on the educational and social landscape, fostering a culture of respect, inclusion, and mutual support.

- ○ **Example**: Community programs and educational initiatives inspired by the values of the Anubhava Mantapa continue to emphasize respect, inclusion, and equality, contributing to the holistic development of individuals and communities.

The Anubhava Mantapa, established by Basavanna, was a revolutionary forum that advanced gender equality and inclusivity in the 12th century. By welcoming all individuals and challenging rigid social hierarchies, it created a platform for open and egalitarian discourse. Key female figures like Akka Mahadevi and other Sharanas played vital roles in shaping the spiritual and cultural ethos of the Lingayat community. The Anubhava Mantapa's legacy continues to inspire modern movements and educational institutions, promoting values of respect, inclusion, and equality.

Corporate Governance & Leadership

- *From Kayaka to Boardrooms: How Lingayatism Shapes Corporate Leadership*

- *Lingayat Thinking in the Corporate Sphere: The Intersection of Tradition and Modernity*

- *Embracing Corporate Excellence: The Lingayat Approach*

- *Ethical Leadership in the Corporate World.*

- *Integration of Work and Spirituality*

- *Transperant and Fair AI*

From Kayaka to Boardrooms: How Lingayatism Shapes Corporate Leadership

The adaptability of practicing Lingayats to the corporate world can be attributed to several factors rooted in their cultural and philosophical values:

1. Work Ethic and Values

The core philosophy of Lingayatism emphasizes **"Kayaka" (work)** and **"Dasoha" (service)** as forms of worship. The principle of "Kayakave Kailasa" (Work is Heaven) encourages a strong work ethic and dedication to one's profession2. This value system aligns well with the demands of the corporate world, where hard work, commitment, and ethical conduct are highly valued.

2. Education and Literacy

The Lingayat community places a high emphasis on education and literacy. Historically, they have established and run numerous educational institutions, contributing to a well-educated and skilled population2. This focus on education provides a solid foundation for individuals to excel in professional and corporate environments.

3. Social Equality and Inclusivity

Lingayatism advocates for social equality and rejects caste-based discrimination. This inclusive mindset fosters a culture of meritocracy, where individuals are judged based on their abilities and contributions rather than their social background. Such an environment is conducive to professional growth and success in the corporate world.

4. Community Support and Networking

The strong sense of community and networking within the Lingayat community provides a support system for individuals pursuing careers in the corporate sector. This network can offer mentorship, guidance, and opportunities for professional development, helping individuals navigate and succeed in their careers.

5. Adaptability and Innovation

The philosophical teachings of Lingayatism, which emphasize personal spiritual experiences and direct connections with the divine, encourage adaptability and innovation. These qualities are essential for thriving in the dynamic and ever-changing corporate world, where flexibility and creativity are key to success.

In summary, the values and principles of Lingayatism, such as a strong work ethic, emphasis on education, social equality, community support, and adaptability, contribute to the success of practicing Lingayats in the corporate world. These factors create a conducive environment for professional growth and achievement.

CHAPTER TWENTY

Lingayat Thinking in the Corporate Sphere: The Intersection of Tradition and Modernity

Breaking the Glass Ceiling: The Lingayat Tradition's Contribution to Gender Equality

Despite the presence of certain prejudices and the glass ceiling, the Lingayat community has made significant strides towards gender equality, particularly in the corporate world. This progress can be attributed to several key factors rooted in Lingayat philosophy and values:

1. Historical Advocacy for Gender Equality

The Lingayat tradition, founded by Basavanna in the 12th century, has always emphasized social equality and rejected caste-based discrimination. Basavanna's teachings promoted the idea that work is worship and that everyone, regardless of gender, should have the opportunity to contribute to society. This foundational belief has carried forward into modern times, encouraging gender equality in various spheres, including the corporate world. By advocating for equal opportunities for all individuals, Basavanna's teachings have laid a strong foundation for gender equality, inspiring contemporary efforts to create more inclusive and equitable workplaces.

2. Education and Empowerment

The Lingayat community places a strong emphasis on education and literacy, recognizing them as key drivers of empowerment. This focus on education has empowered women to pursue higher education and professional careers, breaking traditional gender roles and contributing to a more gender-balanced workforce. By providing access to quality education, the Lingayat community has equipped women with the knowledge and skills needed to excel in their careers. Educated women are better positioned to navigate the corporate world, challenge the glass ceiling, and assume leadership roles, thereby contributing to a more diverse and inclusive professional environment.

3. Community Support and Networking

The sense of community and networking within the Lingayat community provides a robust support system for women aspiring to enter the corporate world. Organizations like the International Lingayat Youth Forum (ILYF) offer vocational training, knowledge sharing, and mentorship programs specifically designed to uplift and empower women. These initiatives help women build the skills and confidence needed to succeed in their careers. The strong community bonds and networking opportunities enable women to access valuable resources, guidance, and support, fostering their professional growth and success.

4. Progressive Leadership

Many Lingayat leaders have been at the forefront of advocating for gender equality and women's rights. Their progressive stance and commitment to social justice have created an environment where women can thrive and contribute meaningfully to the corporate sector. These leaders have championed policies and practices that promote gender equality, breaking down barriers and creating pathways for women to advance in their careers. The leadership's dedication to fostering an inclusive culture has been instrumental in promoting gender equality and ensuring that women's contributions are valued and recognized.

5. Cultural Shifts and Modern Values

While traditional values remain important, there has been a cultural shift towards embracing modern values and practices within the Lingayat community. This shift has led to a greater acceptance of gender equality and the recognition of women's contributions in the corporate world. The blending of traditional values with modern principles has created a more inclusive and equitable environment. By adapting to contemporary values while upholding the core teachings of Basavanna, the Lingayat community has demonstrated its commitment to gender equality and inclusivity.

The Lingayat community's commitment to gender equality, education, community support, progressive leadership, and cultural shifts has significantly enabled women to overcome prejudices and the glass ceiling in the corporate world. By fostering an environment that values equality and empowerment, the Lingayat tradition continues to inspire and support women in their professional journeys. The principles of Lingayatism provide a powerful framework for creating inclusive workplaces where everyone has the opportunity to thrive and contribute to collective success.

Embracing Corporate Excellence: The Lingayat Approach

The Lingayat community's approach to corporate excellence is deeply rooted in their cultural and philosophical values. Here are some key aspects that contribute to their success in the corporate world, along with examples:

The Lingayat Way of Life: Catalysts for Better Corporate Success

1. Strong Work Ethic

The principle of "Kayakave Kailasa" (Work is Heaven), propagated by Basavanna, instills a robust work ethic within the Lingayat community. This belief encourages individuals to approach their work with utmost dedication and sincerity, viewing their professional duties as a form of spiritual practice. By embracing this principle, Lingayat individuals often exhibit high levels of productivity and excellence in their careers. Their unwavering commitment to their responsibilities not only enhances personal success but also contributes to the overall efficiency and effectiveness of the organizations they work for.

2. Emphasis on Education

The Lingayat community places immense value on education, recognizing it as a crucial foundation for professional success. This emphasis on education begins at an early age and continues through higher education and beyond, fostering a culture of continuous learning and intellectual growth. By prioritizing education, individuals in the Lingayat community acquire the knowledge and skills needed to excel in their careers. This focus equips them with the tools to navigate complex professional environments, drive innovation, and contribute meaningfully to their respective fields.

3. Social Equality and Inclusivity

Lingayatism is deeply rooted in the principles of social equality and the rejection of caste-based discrimination. This inclusive mindset creates a culture of meritocracy, where individuals are evaluated based on their abilities and contributions rather than their social background. By fostering an environment of equality and inclusivity, the Lingayat community encourages diverse perspectives and talents, leading to more innovative solutions and a more cohesive work environment. This focus on merit and fairness cultivates a sense of belonging and motivation among employees, enhancing overall organizational performance.

4. Community Support and Networking

The strong sense of community within the Lingayat tradition extends into professional realms, providing a robust support system for individuals pursuing careers in the corporate sector. The network of Lingayat professionals offers mentorship, guidance, and opportunities for professional development. This community support fosters collaboration, sharing of knowledge, and mutual growth, enabling individuals to navigate career challenges more effectively and seize opportunities for advancement. The close-knit community bonds enhance professional resilience and success, contributing to a positive and supportive corporate culture.

5. Adaptability and Innovation

The philosophical teachings of Lingayatism encourage adaptability and innovation, qualities that are essential for thriving in the dynamic and ever-changing corporate world. Lingayat individuals are taught to embrace change, think creatively, and seek out new solutions to challenges. This adaptability allows them to stay ahead in competitive environments, while their innovative mindset drives continuous improvement and growth. The ability to adapt and innovate ensures that Lingayat professionals can navigate the complexities of modern business, leading to sustained success and leadership in their fields.

The Lingayat way of life, with its emphasis on strong work ethic, education, social equality, community support, and adaptability, significantly contributes to better outcomes in the corporate sector. By integrating these values into their professional lives, Lingayat individuals not only achieve personal success but also drive organizational excellence. The principles of Lingayatism provide a framework for ethical leadership and effective governance, demonstrating that ancient wisdom can indeed make a profound difference in the modern corporate world.

CHAPTER TWENTY-TWO

Ethical Leadership in the Corporate World

The phrase **"Work is worship to those who seek truth"** encapsulates Basavanna's belief in the sanctity of honest labor and ethical living. In the context of corporate governance, this principle can be applied in several meaningful ways:

1. Ethical Decision-Making
Integrity and Honesty

- **Transparent Practices:** Just as Basavanna emphasized honesty in one's work, corporate leaders must prioritize transparency in their operations and decision-making processes. This includes clear communication with stakeholders, honest financial reporting, and adherence to legal and ethical standards.

- **Example:** A company that practices ethical decision-making, such as following honest accounting practices and ensuring transparency in financial disclosures, builds trust with its shareholders and the public.

2. Accountability and Responsibility
Moral Accountability

- **Responsibility in Leadership**: Leaders in the corporate world must be accountable for their actions and the actions of their organization. This means taking responsibility for both successes and failures, and ensuring that decisions are made in the best interest of all stakeholders.
- **Example**: A CEO who takes responsibility for a company's downturn and works proactively to address the issues, rather than shifting blame, exemplifies this principle.

3. Fair Treatment and Respect
Respect for All Employees

- **Dignity in Labor**: Basavanna's belief in the dignity of all forms of labor translates to fair treatment of all employees, regardless of their role in the organization. This includes fair wages, safe working conditions, and respect for employees' rights.
- **Example**: Companies that provide fair compensation, opportunities for advancement, and a respectful work environment reflect this principle.

4. Continuous Improvement and Growth
Commitment to Excellence

- **Lifelong Learning**: Organizations should foster a culture of continuous improvement and personal growth. This includes investing in employee training and development, encouraging innovation, and striving for excellence in all areas of operation.
- **Example**: A company that regularly updates its training programs and encourages employees to pursue further

education demonstrates a commitment to continuous improvement.

5. Community Service and Social Responsibility
Corporate Social Responsibility (CSR)

- **Giving Back to Society**: Companies should engage in CSR activities that contribute to the welfare of the community and the environment. This aligns with Basavanna's concept of Dasoha, or selfless service, which brings fulfillment through helping others.
- **Example**: A corporation that invests in community development projects, supports environmental sustainability initiatives, and engages in philanthropy embodies this principle.

6. Inclusivity and Diversity
Promoting Equality

- **Diverse Workforce**: Ensuring diversity and inclusion within the organization fosters a culture of equality and respect. Companies should actively promote diversity in hiring, provide equal opportunities for all employees, and create an inclusive work environment.
- **Example**: An organization with initiatives to support gender equality, cultural diversity, and inclusion of underrepresented groups demonstrates this principle in action.

7. Work-Life Balance
Holistic Well-being

- **Employee Well-being**: Companies should prioritize the well-being of their employees by promoting a healthy work-life balance. This includes providing flexible work hours, mental health support, and opportunities for relaxation and recreation.
- **Example**: Companies offering wellness programs, mental health days, and remote work options show a commitment to their employees' overall well-being.

Vachana in Kannada

"ಕಾಯಕವೇಕ್ಕೈಲಾಸ"

Translation in English

"Work is Worship"

This vachana by Basavanna underscores the principle that all work, when done with dedication and integrity, is equivalent to worship. It emphasizes the importance of honest labor and ethical living, aligning perfectly with the corporate governance principle of maintaining core values while embracing innovation.

This Vachana encapsulates the essence of balancing tradition with innovation:

Respecting Established Practices: The phrase "Work is Worship" reflects the importance of respecting and valuing the work we do, which can be seen as preserving established, proven business practices that have contributed to a company's success.

Embracing New Ideas: It also opens the door to viewing work as a dynamic and evolving process, encouraging innovation and the adoption of new technologies to improve efficiency and drive growth.

By integrating this principle into corporate governance, companies can ensure they honor their traditions and core values while remaining open to new ideas and advancements. This balance between tradition and innovation fosters a culture of continuous improvement and ethical growth.

Integrating the principle of "Work is worship to those who seek truth" into corporate governance means creating an environment where ethical behavior, accountability, inclusivity, continuous growth, and social responsibility are paramount. By doing so, companies can foster trust, respect, and loyalty among employees, stakeholders, and the broader community, leading to sustainable success and a positive impact on society.

II. Social Responsibility:

"Dasoha, or Selfless Service, is a Path to Spiritual Fulfillment"

Basavanna's teaching of "Dasoha" emphasizes the importance of selfless service and community welfare as a path to spiritual fulfillment. This principle can be effectively applied in the corporate world through the concept of Corporate Social Responsibility (CSR). Here's how:

1. Understanding Dasoha
Principle of Selfless Service

- **Spiritual Fulfillment:** Dasoha, in the context of Basavanna's teachings, refers to selfless service that is performed without any expectation of reward or recognition. The focus is on the act of giving and serving others as a means of achieving spiritual growth and fulfillment.

- **Community Welfare**: Basavanna believed that serving the community and addressing its needs is a fundamental aspect of living a meaningful and ethical life.

2. Corporate Social Responsibility (CSR)

CSR is a business model that integrates social and environmental concerns into a company's operations and interactions with stakeholders. It aligns well with the principle of Dasoha by promoting selfless service and community welfare in the corporate setting.

Key Aspects of CSR

1. **Environmental Sustainability**

   - **Example**: A company can engage in eco-friendly practices, such as reducing carbon emissions, conserving energy, and promoting recycling. These efforts contribute to environmental sustainability and reflect a commitment to preserving the planet for future generations.
   - Just as Basavanna promoted living in harmony with nature, CSR initiatives that focus on environmental sustainability are like planting trees that will provide shade and nourishment for generations to come.

2. **Community Development**

   - **Example**: Corporations can support community development projects, such as building schools, healthcare centers, and infrastructure in underprivileged areas. This not only improves the quality of life for the community but also fosters goodwill and strengthens the company's relationship with its stakeholders.

- Engaging in community development is like a gardener tending to a community garden, nurturing and cultivating growth for a thriving and vibrant environment.

3. **Employee Welfare**

- **Example**: Companies can implement programs that prioritize employee well-being, such as offering health and wellness programs, providing fair wages, and ensuring safe working conditions. These initiatives demonstrate a commitment to the holistic well-being of employees.
- Just as Basavanna emphasized the importance of respecting all forms of labor, CSR initiatives that focus on employee welfare are like a nurturing caregiver ensuring that everyone under their care thrives and flourishes.

4. **Ethical Business Practices**

- **Example**: Upholding ethical standards in business operations, such as transparency, honesty, and fair dealing, fosters trust and credibility. Companies that prioritize ethical practices are more likely to gain the trust and loyalty of their customers and stakeholders.
- Ethical business practices are like a beacon of light guiding a ship through stormy seas, providing direction and assurance in challenging times.

3. Benefits of Integrating Dasoha in CSR

Enhanced Corporate Reputation

- **Positive Image**: Companies that actively engage in CSR initiatives and practice selfless service build a positive reputation, which can lead to increased customer loyalty and trust.

Employee Satisfaction and Retention

- **Motivated Workforce**: Employees are more likely to feel motivated and committed to a company that demonstrates a genuine concern for their well-being and the well-being of the community.

Community Support

- **Strong Relationships**: By addressing community needs and contributing to social welfare, companies can build strong and supportive relationships with the communities in which they operate.

"One who lights a lamp and offers a small gift,One who conducts many sacrifices and rituals.Among these, who is the real victor?It is the humble one who lives a life of selfless service in Basavanna's Linga."

was written by Basavanna, a prominent saint and philosopher of the Lingayat tradition. His vachanas emphasize principles such as selfless service (Dasoha), ethical living, and social equality. This particular vachana highlights the value of humble service over grand rituals, aligning with Basavanna's teachings that true spiritual fulfillment comes from sincere acts of service.

Integrating Basavanna's principle of Dasoha into corporate governance through CSR initiatives allows companies to align their operations with ethical and social values. By focusing on selfless service, community welfare, and environmental sustainability, corporations can achieve not only business success but also contribute to the greater good of society, embodying the true spirit of Dasoha.

III. Inclusivity and Equality

"All are Equal in the Eyes of the Divine"
Basavanna's teaching that "All are equal in the eyes of the divine" reflects his firm rejection of the caste system and his advocacy for social equality. This principle can be profoundly influential when applied to corporate governance through the promotion of diversity and inclusion in the workplace. Here are several ways to implement this principle:
1. Creating a Diverse Workforce
Inclusive Hiring Practices

- Equal Opportunity: Companies should ensure that their hiring practices are inclusive and provide equal opportunities for candidates from diverse backgrounds, regardless of race, gender, ethnicity, religion, or disability.
- Example: Implementing blind recruitment processes to eliminate unconscious bias in hiring decisions and ensuring diverse interview panels can help create a more inclusive hiring process.

Representation at All Levels

- Balanced Leadership: Ensuring representation of diverse groups at all levels of the organization, including leadership positions, is crucial. This demonstrates the company's commitment to diversity and sets an example for the rest of the workforce.
- Example: Large Companies have diversity initiatives to increase representation of women and minorities in leadership roles.

2. Fostering an Inclusive Culture
Training and Awareness Programs

- Diversity Training: Providing training programs that educate employees about the importance of diversity and inclusion, and how to recognize and overcome unconscious biases.
- Example: Hosting workshops and seminars on cultural competence, anti-discrimination, and inclusive leadership can foster a more inclusive culture.

Employee Resource Groups (ERGs)

- Support Networks: Establishing ERGs for different demographic groups, such as women, and employees with disabilities, can provide support, advocacy, and a sense of community.
- Example: Large Companies have ERGs that focus on creating an inclusive environment and advocating for the needs of diverse employee groups.

3. Implementing Inclusive Policies
Equal Benefits and Opportunities

- Inclusive Policies: Developing and enforcing policies that ensure equal benefits and opportunities for all employees, such as equal pay, parental leave, and flexible work arrangements.
- Example: Offering gender-neutral parental leave policies and ensuring equal pay for equal work regardless of gender or background.

Zero Tolerance for Discrimination

- Anti-Discrimination Policies: Implementing strict anti-discrimination policies and procedures for reporting and addressing any incidents of discrimination or harassment in the workplace.
- Example: Establishing a clear process for employees to report discrimination and ensuring swift and fair resolution of complaints.

4. Measuring and Celebrating Diversity
Diversity Metrics and Goals

- Tracking Progress: Setting diversity goals and regularly measuring progress through diversity metrics, such as representation, pay equity, and employee satisfaction.
- Example: Many Companies publicly share their diversity metrics and progress towards their diversity and inclusion goals.

Recognition and Celebration

- Cultural Celebrations: Recognizing and celebrating diverse cultures, backgrounds, and perspectives through company-wide events, cultural awareness days, and inclusive holidays.

5. Inclusive Leadership
Leading by Example

- Role Models: Leaders should exemplify inclusive behavior and set the tone for the organization. They should actively promote diversity, challenge biases, and create an environment where all employees feel valued and included.

Vachana in Kannada

"ಅವನು ಬಡವಿರಲಿ, ಧನಿಕನಿರಲಿ, ಅವನು ಶೂದ್ರನಿರಲಿ, ಬ್ರಾಹ್ಮಣನಿರಲಿ, ಕಳ್ಳನಿರಲಿ, ಸಜ್ಜನನಿರಲಿ, ಚಿದಂಬರವು ಅವನ ಸೊಟ್ಟಿನು ಕಾಣಬಲ್ಲ. ಇಂತವರೆಲ್ಲರನು ಕೊರೆದು ಕೋಡದಂತ ಬೇಡ. ಅವನು ಶ್ರೀಬಸವಣ್ಣನ ಲಿಂಗದಲ್ಲಿ ಎಲ್ಲಾ ಸಮನಿರಲಿ."

Translation in English

"Whether he is poor or rich, whether he is a Shudra or a Brahmin, whether he is a thief or a saint, Chidambara sees only the essence within. Do not cut down or despise any of them. In the Linga of Sri Basavanna, all are equal."

This vachana emphasizes Basavanna's teaching that everyone is equal in the eyes of the divine, regardless of their social status, caste, or actions. It encourages us to see the inherent worth in every individual and to treat everyone with respect and dignity.

By integrating Basavanna's principle of "All are equal in the eyes of the divine" into corporate governance, companies can create a workplace that values diversity, promotes inclusion, and ensures equal opportunities for all employees. This not only aligns with ethical values but also contributes to a more innovative, productive, and harmonious work environment.

CHAPTER TWENTY-THREE

Continuous Learning and Growth

"The Pursuit of Knowledge is a Lifelong Journey"

Basavanna's teaching, "The pursuit of knowledge is a lifelong journey," underscores the importance of continuous learning and personal growth. In a corporate context, fostering a culture of continuous improvement and innovation is vital for maintaining a competitive edge and ensuring long-term success. Here's how this principle can be integrated into corporate governance:

1. Fostering a Culture of Continuous Improvement
Encouraging Lifelong Learning

- Organizational Mindset: Companies should cultivate an organizational mindset that values and promotes lifelong learning. This involves creating an environment where learning is seen as an ongoing process, essential for both personal and professional development.

2. Employee Training and Development Programs
Comprehensive Training Initiatives

- Skill Enhancement: Offering a range of training programs that focus on enhancing both technical and soft skills is crucial. These programs can include workshops, seminars, online courses, and certifications.

Onboarding and Orientation

- Effective Onboarding: Implementing robust onboarding programs to ensure new hires quickly acquire the necessary skills and knowledge to perform their roles effectively.

3. Encouraging Innovation
Innovation Labs and Hackathons

- Creativity and Experimentation: Establishing innovation labs or organizing hackathons can encourage employees to experiment with new ideas and technologies. These initiatives foster a culture of creativity and problem-solving.

Open Innovation Platforms

- Collaborative Innovation: Utilizing open innovation platforms where employees, customers, and external partners can collaborate on new ideas and solutions.

4. Leadership Development
Mentorship Programs

- Knowledge Transfer: Implementing mentorship programs where experienced employees mentor newer or less experienced staff, facilitating knowledge transfer and professional development.

Leadership Training

- Developing Leaders: Providing leadership training to equip managers and potential leaders with the skills needed to lead teams effectively and drive organizational success.

5. Leveraging Technology for Learning
E-Learning Platforms

- Accessible Learning: Utilizing e-learning platforms and digital resources to provide employees with access to training materials anytime, anywhere. This flexibility supports continuous learning.

Gamification and Interactive Learning

- Engaging Training Methods: Incorporating gamification and interactive elements into training programs to make learning more engaging and effective.

6. Performance Management and Feedback
Regular Feedback

- Continuous Improvement: Implementing regular performance reviews and feedback sessions to help employees identify areas for improvement and set goals for development.

Personal Development Plans

- Goal Setting: Encouraging employees to create personal development plans that outline their career goals and the steps needed to achieve them.

Integrating Basavanna's principle of continuous learning and personal growth into corporate governance means creating a culture that values ongoing education, innovation, and improvement. By investing in employee training and development programs, fostering a culture of innovation, and leveraging technology for learning, companies can ensure their workforce remains skilled and adaptable to changing market conditions, ultimately driving long-term success.

Balancing Tradition and Innovation

"Respect the Wisdom of the Past While Embracing the Possibilities of the Future"

Basavanna's teaching to "Respect the wisdom of the past while embracing the possibilities of the future" emphasizes the importance of balancing tradition with innovation. In the context of corporate governance, this principle can guide companies in maintaining their core values and proven practices while being open to new ideas and technologies that can drive growth and efficiency. Here's how this balance can be achieved:

1. Valuing Established Business Practices

Core Values and Ethical Standards

- **Preserving Integrity**: Companies should continue to uphold their core values and ethical standards that have built their reputation and trust over time. This includes maintaining transparent practices, ethical decision-making, and a commitment to social responsibility.

Proven Operational Processes

- **Efficiency and Reliability**: Established business practices that have proven to be efficient and reliable should be retained. These practices form the foundation upon which new innovations can be built.

2. Embracing Innovation and New Technologies
Adopting Cutting-Edge Technologies

- **Staying Competitive**: To remain competitive, companies must embrace new technologies that can enhance efficiency, productivity, and customer experience. This includes adopting digital transformation strategies, leveraging big data, and integrating AI and machine learning.

Encouraging a Culture of Innovation

- **Fostering Creativity**: Companies should foster a culture of innovation by encouraging employees to think creatively, experiment with new ideas, and take calculated risks. This can be achieved through innovation labs, hackathons, and an open innovation platform.

3. Balancing Tradition and Innovation in Decision-Making
Strategic Planning

- **Integrating Both Aspects**: Strategic planning should integrate both traditional wisdom and innovative solutions. This involves assessing the potential impact of new technologies while considering the company's existing strengths and values.

Inclusive Leadership

- **Diverse Perspectives**: Leadership teams should include members with diverse backgrounds and perspectives, ensuring that decisions are informed by both historical knowledge and innovative thinking.

4. Continuous Learning and Adaptation
Employee Training and Development

- **Lifelong Learning**: Companies should invest in continuous learning and development programs for employees to keep them updated with the latest industry trends and technological advancements while reinforcing the company's core values.

Feedback and Improvement

- **Iterative Improvement**: Embracing a feedback culture where employees and stakeholders can provide insights on existing practices and suggest improvements ensures continuous refinement and adaptation.

5. Preserving Cultural Heritage
Corporate Traditions

- **Honoring Legacy**: Companies should honor their cultural heritage and traditions that have contributed to their identity and success. This includes celebrating milestones, recognizing long-term employees, and maintaining rituals that reinforce the company's values.

Knowledge Sharing

- **Intergenerational Knowledge**: Facilitating knowledge sharing between experienced employees and newer generations ensures that valuable insights and lessons from the past are not lost while encouraging fresh ideas.

"Knowing the old and embracing the new, Let us go to Kailasa, O Kallovayya. Stone stands still, is cut and sculpted, but it remains one, do not doubt or worry. Basavanna shows the way, should we not respect the fruit while worshipping the tree?"

This vachana by Basavanna highlights the importance of understanding and valuing past wisdom while being open to new ideas and possibilities. It encourages a balance between tradition and innovation, suggesting that both are essential for growth and progress.

Balancing tradition with innovation is essential for sustainable corporate governance. By respecting established business practices and core values while embracing new ideas and technologies, companies can navigate the complexities of modern markets, drive growth, and maintain their competitive edge. Integrating Basavanna's teachings into corporate governance ensures that companies remain rooted in ethical principles while continuously evolving and innovating.

VI. Stakeholder Engagement

"Listen to the Voices of the People"

Basavanna's **Anubhava Mantapa** was an innovative and revolutionary forum that embodied the principle of listening to the voices of the people. Established in the

12th century, it served as a platform for open discussion, collective decision-making, and the sharing of diverse ideas and perspectives. Here's an elaborate exploration of this principle and its relevance in corporate governance:

Anubhava Mantapa: A Historical Perspective
Inclusive and Open Forum

- **Diverse Participation**: Anubhava Mantapa brought together individuals from various backgrounds, including saints, philosophers, poets, and common people, irrespective of caste, gender, or social status. This inclusivity ensured that a wide range of voices and perspectives were heard and respected.
- **Collective Decision-Making**: The forum encouraged open dialogue and collective decision-making, allowing participants to discuss and resolve social, ethical, and spiritual issues collaboratively.

Sharing Knowledge and Wisdom

- **Exchange of Ideas**: Anubhava Mantapa facilitated the exchange of ideas and knowledge, promoting intellectual and spiritual growth. Participants were encouraged to share their experiences, insights, and wisdom, contributing to a collective understanding and enrichment.
- **Vachanas as a Medium**: The discussions and teachings from Anubhava Mantapa were often expressed through Vachanas, a form of devotional poetry that encapsulated the principles of ethical living, social equality, and devotion to Shiva.

Relevance in Corporate Governance

Employee Engagement and Inclusion
Inclusive Decision-Making

- **Open Communication Channels**: Just as Anubhava Mantapa valued the voices of all participants, companies should establish open communication channels that allow employees at all levels to share their ideas, concerns, and feedback. This can be achieved through regular town hall meetings, suggestion boxes, and open-door policies.

Collaborative Problem-Solving

- **Team Collaboration**: Encouraging collaborative problem-solving and decision-making within teams helps ensure that diverse perspectives are considered. This approach can lead to more innovative solutions and better decision-making.

Stakeholder Engagement
Listening to Stakeholders

- **Inclusive Stakeholder Engagement**: Companies should actively engage with all stakeholders, including employees, customers, suppliers, and the community. This involves listening to their needs, concerns, and feedback and incorporating these insights into decision-making processes.

Community Involvement

- **Corporate Social Responsibility (CSR)**: Engaging with the community through CSR initiatives aligns with

Basavanna's principle of selfless service and community welfare. Companies can support community development projects, environmental sustainability, and educational programs.

Continuous Improvement and Innovation
Feedback and Improvement

- **Continuous Feedback Loop**: Establishing a continuous feedback loop where employees and stakeholders can provide insights and suggestions for improvement helps companies stay agile and responsive to changing needs and market conditions.

Leadership and Governance
Inclusive Leadership

- **Empathetic Leadership**: Leaders should embody the principles of empathy and active listening, ensuring that all voices are heard and valued. This fosters a culture of trust, respect, and collaboration.

Basavanna's Anubhava Mantapa serves as an enduring example of the power of inclusive dialogue and collective decision-making. By integrating the principles of listening to the voices of the people into corporate governance, companies can create an environment that values diverse perspectives, fosters innovation, and promotes ethical and inclusive decision-making. This approach not only enhances organizational performance but also contributes to a more just and equitable society.

CHAPTER TWENTY-FOUR

Integration of Work and Spirituality

Unified Life Approach

- **Holistic View**

Basavanna emphasized the unity of the sacred and secular, advocating that there should be no separation between the two. He taught that by viewing work as a form of worship, individuals can integrate their spiritual and daily lives. This perspective allows people to find holiness in their everyday activities, transforming routine tasks into acts of devotion. By considering work as an extension of their spiritual practice, individuals can approach their professional responsibilities with a sense of reverence and purpose. This holistic view fosters a deeper connection between one's faith and daily life, promoting a balanced and fulfilling existence.

Inner Devotion

Engaging in honest work with dedication and integrity is viewed as a direct form of devotion to the divine in Basavanna's teachings. This approach encourages individuals to infuse their daily tasks with a sense of purpose and reverence, seeing their professional duties as opportunities to honor their spiritual beliefs. By committing to ethical behavior and sincere effort in all endeavors, individuals demonstrate their devotion not just through prayer or ritual but through their actions and contributions. This inner devotion transforms mundane activities into meaningful expressions of faith, reinforcing the importance of integrity and purpose in both personal and professional spheres.

A Glimpse into Basavanna's Era and His Revolutionary Teachings

Global Context of Basavanna's Era

Basavanna, a 12th-century philosopher and statesman, lived during a period of profound social, economic, and cultural change. The 12th century globally was marked by the rise of powerful empires and the spread of major religions. In Europe, this was the time of the High Middle Ages, characterized by the growth of cities, the establishment of universities, and the Crusades. In the Islamic world, the Seljuk Empire was a dominant force, and the Islamic Golden Age saw significant advancements in science, philosophy, and the arts. In East Asia, the Song Dynasty in China was experiencing economic prosperity and cultural flourishing.

In this backdrop, Basavanna emerged as a visionary leader in the Indian subcontinent, specifically in the region of Karnataka. He founded the Lingayat movement, which advocated for social equality, the rejection of caste-based discrimination, and the dignity of all forms of labor. His teachings were revolutionary, challenging the deeply entrenched social hierarchies and norms of his time.

Elevating Labor: A Revolutionary Concept

Basavanna's teachings elevated all forms of honest labor, regardless of social status or occupation, to the level of worship. This principle, known as "Kayakave Kailasa" (Work is Heaven), dignified even the most humble professions. By considering work as worship, Basavanna instilled a sense of purpose and reverence in daily activities, transforming routine tasks into acts of devotion. This approach was revolutionary because it recognized the intrinsic value of every individual's contribution to society, irrespective of their job or social standing.

In an era when labor, especially manual labor, was often looked down upon, Basavanna's emphasis on the dignity of work was a radical departure from the norm. His teachings encouraged individuals to take pride in their work, fostering a culture of respect and appreciation for all forms of labor. This principle not only elevated the status of workers but also promoted a more egalitarian and inclusive society.

Combating Discrimination: Promoting Equality and Respect

Basavanna's teachings also played a crucial role in combating caste and class discrimination. By rejecting the rigid caste system and advocating for social equality, he promoted the idea that everyone, regardless of their social background, should be treated with respect and dignity. His principles encouraged the breaking down of barriers that separated people based on their birth and occupation, fostering a culture of meritocracy where individuals were judged by their abilities and contributions.

This principle was far ahead of its time, as it laid the groundwork for a more inclusive and just society. By advocating for the equal treatment of all workers, Basavanna's teachings challenged the prevailing social norms and hierarchies, paving the way for social reforms and greater acceptance of diversity.

In summary, Basavanna's era was a time of significant social and cultural change, both globally and locally. His teachings on elevating labor and combating discrimination were revolutionary, challenging the deeply entrenched social norms of his time. By dignifying all forms of honest labor and promoting equality and respect for all workers, Basavanna's principles laid the foundation for a more inclusive and just society. These teachings continue to inspire and guide contemporary efforts to create equitable and respectful work environments, demonstrating that ancient wisdom can indeed have a profound impact on modern life.

Ethical Conduct

Honesty and Integrity

Ethical Actions

Emphasizing ethical behavior in one's work ensures that individuals act with honesty, fairness, and integrity in all their dealings. Basavanna's teachings advocate for transparent and ethical actions in every aspect of life, particularly in the professional realm. By adhering to these principles, individuals create a trustworthy environment, fostering mutual respect and collaboration. Ethical actions build a solid foundation for personal and professional relationships, ensuring that dealings are conducted with a high level of integrity. This not only enhances one's reputation but also contributes to a culture of honesty and fairness within the organization.

Moral Accountability

Viewing work as worship encourages individuals to be morally accountable, ensuring their actions align with their values and principles. Basavanna's concept of "Kayakave

Kailasa" (Work is Heaven) instills a sense of purpose and devotion in one's professional duties, prompting individuals to act with a clear conscience. Moral accountability means taking responsibility for one's actions and decisions, striving to maintain high ethical standards, and being answerable for the outcomes. This principle fosters a sense of inner integrity and discipline, guiding individuals to make decisions that reflect their core values and ethical beliefs, ultimately leading to greater personal and professional fulfillment.

Community and Service

Concept of Dasoha: Serving Society

Basavanna's concept of "Dasoha" (service) complements the idea that work is worship. This principle encourages individuals to serve the community through their work, contributing to the greater good. By embracing Dasoha, individuals view their professional roles not just as jobs but as opportunities to make a positive impact on society. This service-oriented mindset fosters a culture of altruism and generosity, where individuals are motivated to use their skills and resources for the benefit of others. The act of serving the community through one's work instills a sense of fulfillment and purpose, reinforcing the belief that every contribution, no matter how small, is valuable and meaningful.

Building Equity: Promoting Social Harmony

Ethical work practices help build a more just and equitable society, reflecting Basavanna's vision of social harmony. By promoting fairness, inclusivity, and respect for all individuals, these practices combat social inequality and discrimination. Basavanna's teachings emphasize the importance of treating everyone with dignity and respect, regardless of their social status or background. By integrating these values into the workplace, organizations can create environments that foster equity and social justice. This not only enhances the well-being of individuals but also contributes to a cohesive and harmonious society, where everyone's contributions are recognized and valued.

The teachings of Basavanna, centered on honesty, integrity, service, and equity, provide a powerful framework for both personal and professional life. By emphasizing ethical actions, moral accountability, community service, and social equity, these principles guide individuals to lead lives of purpose and integrity. The integration of these values into daily activities and professional responsibilities fosters a culture of respect, trust, and harmony, reflecting Basavanna's timeless vision of a just and compassionate society. Through these teachings, individuals can find fulfillment and meaning in their work, contributing positively to the world around them.

Personal Fulfillment

Sense of Accomplishment

- **Meaning in Tasks**: Treating work as worship provides a deeper sense of fulfillment and satisfaction, as individuals find meaning and purpose in their daily tasks.
- **Spiritual Growth**: This approach fosters personal spiritual growth, as individuals align their actions with their spiritual values and seek truth through their work.

Examples and Similes

Craftsman and Devotion

- **Meticulous Craftsmanship**: Just as a craftsman meticulously shapes a piece of wood into a beautiful work of art, individuals should approach their work with the same dedication and love, finding spiritual fulfillment in their efforts.

Farmer and Harvest

- **Caring for Crops**: Like a farmer who tends to his crops with care and devotion, knowing that the harvest is both his livelihood and offering to the divine, individuals should see their work as a sacred duty that nourishes both themselves and society.

Basavanna's teaching that **"Work is worship to those who seek truth"** encourages individuals to find spiritual significance in their daily activities, promoting ethical living, respect for all forms of labor, and personal fulfillment. His principles remain a guiding light, helping us to lead lives of integrity and purpose.

Ethical Development and Use
Integrity and Responsibility

- **Transparent and Fair AI**: Basavanna's emphasis on ethical living and honesty urges AI and ML practitioners to develop and use technology responsibly. This includes ensuring transparency, accountability, and fairness in AI systems.
- **Avoiding Bias**: Just as Basavanna fought against social discrimination, developers should strive to eliminate biases in AI algorithms that could perpetuate inequality and injustice. Ensuring diverse and unbiased data sets is key to achieving this goal.

Inclusivity and Accessibility
Democratizing Technology

- **Equal Access to AI**: Basavanna's vision of social equality aligns with the goal of making AI and ML technologies accessible to all, regardless of socioeconomic status. Efforts should be made to ensure that these technologies benefit the broader society, not just a privileged few.
- **Diverse Perspectives**: Involving people from diverse backgrounds in the development and deployment of AI ensures that these technologies address a wide range of needs and perspectives. This approach promotes inclusivity and innovation.

Personal and Social Responsibility
Accountability in Innovation

- **Ethical Considerations**: Basavanna's teachings on ethical conduct remind us that with great technological power comes great responsibility. Innovators should consider the societal impact of their work and strive to create solutions that promote the common good.
- **Community Engagement**: Encouraging community participation in discussions about AI and ML can help ensure that these technologies are developed and used in ways that align with societal values and needs. Engaging with diverse stakeholders can lead to more ethical and socially responsible innovations.

Continuous Learning and Adaptation
Lifelong Learning

- **Adapting to Change**: Basavanna's advocacy for continuous learning resonates with the need for ongoing education and adaptation in the rapidly evolving field of AI and ML. Staying updated with the latest advancements and ethical standards is crucial for practitioners.
- **Critical Thinking**: Just as Basavanna promoted open dialogue and critical thinking, practitioners should critically evaluate the implications of AI technologies and engage in thoughtful discussions about their ethical and social impact. This approach fosters responsible innovation and ethical decision-making.

Sustainability and Harmony
Sustainable Development

- **Eco-friendly AI Solutions**: Basavanna's teachings on living harmoniously with nature highlight the importance of developing AI solutions that are environmentally sustainable and contribute to the well-being of the planet. Embracing green technologies and reducing the environmental footprint of AI systems align with his principles.
- **Balancing Progress and Nature**: Ensuring that technological advancements do not come at the expense of the environment is essential. This balance reflects Basavanna's vision of harmonious coexistence with nature.

Basavanna's teachings offer timeless wisdom that remains relevant even in the age of AI and ML. His principles of ethical living, social equality, and continuous learning provide valuable guidance for developing and using these technologies responsibly. By integrating his teachings, we can create a more just, inclusive, and sustainable technological future.

Ethical AI for Good

- **Harnessing Technology for Positive Change**: AI and ML should be utilized to address global challenges such as climate change, healthcare, education, and social justice. By aligning with Basavanna's teachings, these technologies can be directed towards creating a positive impact on society.

Examples and Similes

- **Bias in Algorithms**

  - **Example**: Removing biases from AI algorithms is critical to ensure fairness and equality. Developers must be vigilant in identifying and eliminating these biases to prevent discrimination.
  - **Simile**: Just as Basavanna opposed social discrimination, AI practitioners should act like skilled gardeners, carefully removing weeds (biases) to ensure a fair and fruitful garden (algorithm).

- **Community Engagement in AI**

  - **Example**: Engaging diverse voices in the development of AI technologies ensures that they address a wide range of needs and perspectives. This inclusivity leads to more robust and equitable solutions.

- **Simile**: Involving diverse voices in AI development is akin to Basavanna's Anubhava Mantapa, where open dialogue and inclusivity led to richer, more meaningful insights.

By integrating Basavanna's teachings into the development and use of AI and ML, the younger generation can ensure that these powerful technologies serve as tools for ethical progress, social equality, and global well-being. The principles of integrity, inclusivity, and responsible innovation inspired by Basavanna's teachings remain as relevant today as they were in the 12th century.

CHAPTER TWENTY-FIVE

Transparent and Fair AI: Guiding Principles from Basavanna's Teachings

Ethical Living and Honesty

Basavanna's teachings on ethical living and honesty serve as a profound guide for AI and Machine Learning (ML) practitioners. In an era where technology increasingly shapes our daily lives, adhering to these principles is crucial. By grounding their work in ethical behavior and transparency, AI practitioners can ensure that the technology they develop and deploy is used responsibly and ethically. This approach fosters trust and confidence among users, paving the way for more equitable and beneficial AI systems.

Transparency in AI Systems

Transparency is a cornerstone of ethical AI. Basavanna's emphasis on honesty aligns with the need for AI systems to be transparent in their operations and decision-making processes. Practitioners should strive to make AI algorithms and their functioning understandable to users, regulators, and other stakeholders. This involves clear documentation, open communication about how data is used, and providing explanations for AI-driven decisions. Transparency ensures that AI systems are not black boxes but tools whose workings are accessible and comprehensible, fostering trust and accountability.

Accountability in AI Development

Accountability is essential in the development and deployment of AI systems. Basavanna's teachings urge individuals to take responsibility for their actions, which is equally applicable to AI practitioners. Developers and organizations must be accountable for the performance, impact, and potential biases of their AI systems. This includes conducting thorough testing, auditing algorithms for biases, and implementing mechanisms for addressing issues that arise. By embracing accountability, practitioners can ensure that AI systems are fair, reliable, and aligned with ethical standards.

Fairness in AI Practices

Fairness is a critical aspect of ethical AI, deeply rooted in Basavanna's advocacy for social equality. AI practitioners must ensure that their systems do not perpetuate or amplify existing biases and discrimination. This involves using diverse and representative data sets, designing algorithms that treat all users equitably, and actively working to mitigate biases. Fair AI systems promote inclusivity and social justice, reflecting Basavanna's vision of a society where everyone is treated with respect and dignity.

Integrating Ethical Principles in AI Development

Integrating Basavanna's ethical principles into AI development involves a holistic approach that encompasses transparency, accountability, and fairness. Practitioners should adopt a comprehensive ethical framework that guides their work at every stage of the AI lifecycle, from data collection and algorithm design to deployment and monitoring. This framework should include:

Ethical Audits: Regularly auditing AI systems to identify and address ethical concerns.

User Education: Educating users about how AI systems work and how their data is used.

Bias Mitigation: Implementing strategies to detect and reduce biases in AI models.

Stakeholder Engagement: Involving diverse stakeholders in the design and evaluation of AI systems to ensure they meet ethical standards.

Basavanna's teachings on ethical living and honesty provide valuable guidance for developing and using AI responsibly. By ensuring transparency, accountability, and fairness in AI systems, practitioners can create technology that serves the greater good and promotes social harmony. Adopting these principles helps build trust, fosters inclusivity, and ensures that AI contributes positively to society. In essence, Basavanna's vision of ethical living can inspire and shape the future of AI, making it a force for good in our increasingly digital world.

Contemporary Relevance

•

Kalyana Kranthi: A Landmark in Basavanna's Life.

•

The Lingayath Community's Hardships and Resilience During the Kalyan Kranthi Period.

•

Basavanna: Resonance with Gen Z, Digital Activism, and Social Justice

CHAPTER TWENTY-SIX

Kalyana Kranthi: A Landmark in Basavanna's Life.

Kalyana Kranthi is a significant historical event in the life of Basavanna, the founder of the Lingayat sect. Here's a detailed explanation of this landmark event:

Administrative Role

- Kalyana Region: Basavanna served in the administration of the Kalyana region, now known as Basavana Bagewadi in Karnataka. His role in the governance of this region provided him with a platform to implement his visionary social and religious reforms.
- Social Reforms: During his tenure, Basavanna initiated a series of progressive reforms aimed at creating a more just and inclusive society. He vehemently opposed the caste system and promoted social equality, ensuring that all individuals had the opportunity to participate in religious and societal affairs.

Religious Reforms

- Lingayat Sect: Basavanna's efforts in Kalyana led to the establishment of the Lingayat sect, which emphasized personal devotion to Lord Shiva, the rejection of caste distinctions, and the importance of ethical living. His teachings and reforms laid the foundation for a spiritual movement that sought to democratize religious practices and empower the marginalized.
- Anubhava Mantapa: One of Basavanna's most notable contributions during this period was the establishment of the Anubhava Mantapa, a spiritual and philosophical forum where individuals from diverse backgrounds could engage in open dialogue and share their spiritual experiences.

Legacy of Kalyana Kranthi

- Enduring Influence: The Kalyana Kranthi symbolizes Basavanna's relentless pursuit of social justice and spiritual awakening. His reforms not only transformed the region of Kalyana but also had a lasting impact on the spiritual landscape of Karnataka and beyond.
- Inspiration for Future Generations: The principles of equality, inclusivity, and devotion championed by Basavanna continue to inspire modern movements and social reforms. His legacy is a testament to the enduring power of visionary leadership and spiritual commitment.

Sharana Haralayya: A Beacon of Equality and Devotion

Sharana Haralayya, also known as Guru Haralayya, was a 12th-century saint and poet in the Lingayat tradition. His life and contributions are a testament to the transformative power of the Sharana movement led by Basavanna. Here are the expanded details about his life and legacy:

Early Life

- Birth: Haralayya was born into the Chamar community in Basavakalyan, Karnataka, a region that became the epicenter of the Sharana movement.
- Profession: Despite his humble beginnings as a cobbler, Haralayya's spiritual journey led him to become a revered saint and poet.

Contributions

- Anubhava Mantapa: Haralayya joined the Anubhava Mantapa, a revolutionary spiritual forum established by Basavanna. This forum welcomed individuals from all castes and backgrounds, fostering an environment of inclusivity and open dialogue.
- Poetry: He composed Vachana poems, which are brief, pithy pieces of poetic prose written in Kannada. His poetry reflected his deep spiritual insights and his commitment to the principles of the Sharana movement.
- Social Reforms: Haralayya was a staunch advocate for social equality and worked tirelessly to break down caste barriers. His efforts were instrumental in promoting the values of equality and justice within the Lingayat community.

Legacy

- Miracles: Haralayya is known for performing miracles, including healing the leprosy of Madhavarasa, a

Brahmin minister. This act of compassion and healing further solidified his reputation as a saint with divine powers.

- Marriage: Haralayya's son, Sheelavantha, was married to Lavanya, the daughter of Madhavarasa. This marriage symbolized the breaking down of caste barriers and the unity of different social strata.

- Opposition and Tragic End: The marriage faced strong opposition from Bijjala II, the ruler of the Southern Kalachuris. Haralayya and his family were ultimately killed by Bijjala II due to the ruler's resistance to the social reforms and the Sharana movement2.

The True Essence of the Opposition to Basavanna and the Sharana Movement

The opposition to Basavanna and the Sharana movement was rooted in the entrenched caste system and the rigid social hierarchies of the time. Basavanna's vision of a society based on equality, justice, and devotion to the divine challenged the traditional power structures and threatened the status quo3. The Sharana movement, with its emphasis on inclusivity and social reform, posed a direct threat to the Brahmanical orthodoxy and the ruling elite.

Impact of the Opposition

- Resistance to Change: The ruling class, including Bijjala II, resisted the Sharana movement's call for social equality and the dismantling of caste barriers. This resistance was driven by a desire to maintain their power and control over the societal order3.

- Tragic Consequences: The opposition led to tragic consequences, including the persecution and martyrdom of key figures like Haralayya and his family.

Despite the violence and opposition, the Sharana movement continued to inspire and mobilize people towards the ideals of equality and devotion3.

Sharana Haralayya's life and contributions highlight the transformative power of the Sharana movement and the challenges faced by those who dared to challenge the status quo. His legacy, along with that of other Sharanas, continues to inspire future generations to strive for a more just and inclusive society.

CHAPTER TWENTY-SEVEN

The Lingayat Community's Hardships and Resilience During the Kalyan Kranthi Period

The Kalyan Kranthi period marks a dark and tumultuous chapter in the history of the Lingayath community. During this time, the community faced severe persecution, forced migration, and the destruction of their rich literary heritage. Despite these adversities, the resilience and determination of the Sharanas ensured the preservation and continuation of their faith and teachings.

Destruction of Vachana Sahitya Literature

Loss of Literary Heritage

- Vachana Sahitya: The Vachanas, composed by Basavanna, Akka Mahadevi, Allam Prabhu, and other Sharanas, were a treasure trove of spiritual wisdom, poetic beauty, and social critique. These literary works played a crucial role in conveying the principles of Lingayatism, including devotion to Shiva, social equality, and ethical living.

- Tragic Destruction: During the Kalyan Kranthi period, the destruction of Vachana Sahitya literature by orthodox elements was a profound loss. The systematic efforts to erase these texts aimed to suppress the revolutionary ideas that challenged the existing social order and promoted a more inclusive and egalitarian society.

Massacre and Forced Displacement

- Severe Opposition: The Sharanas, including prominent figures like Channabasavanna and Akka Mahadevi, faced intense persecution from the ruling elite and orthodox Brahmins who resisted their progressive ideas. The opposition to the Sharana movement was driven by a desire to maintain the rigid caste hierarchy and traditional power structures.
- Massacre of Sharanas: Many Sharanas were brutally massacred during this period, and their communities were targeted for their association with Basava Dharma. The violence and persecution were aimed at extinguishing the spirit of reform and resistance embodied by the Sharanas.

Forced Migration

- Exodus from Kalyan: As a result of the persecution, many Sharanas were forced to flee from Kalyan (modern-day Basavana Bagewadi, Karnataka). This exodus led them to seek refuge in various regions, including Ulavi in the Western Ghats and Shrishaila in Andhra Pradesh.

- Preservation of Faith: Despite the hardships of migration, the Sharanas carried with them their unwavering faith and commitment to the principles of Lingayatism. They continued to practice and propagate their beliefs, ensuring the survival of their spiritual and cultural heritage.

Preservation of Teachings and Cultural Heritage Underground Efforts

- Secret Preservation: In the face of destruction and persecution, the Lingayath community employed secretive methods to preserve their teachings. Manuscripts of Vachanas were hidden, and oral traditions were maintained to safeguard the knowledge and wisdom of their saints.
- Oral Transmission: The community relied heavily on oral transmission of teachings, passing down the Vachanas and philosophical ideas from one generation to the next. This ensured that the core principles of Lingayatism were not lost, even in the absence of written records.

Refuge and Resilience

- Sanctuaries in Ulavi and Shrishaila: The regions of Ulavi and Shrishaila provided sanctuaries for the displaced Sharanas. These places became centers of spiritual and cultural rejuvenation, where the community could rebuild and continue their practices.

- Continued Inspiration: The spirit of resilience and devotion exhibited by the Sharanas during their exile inspired future generations. Their ability to adapt and persevere in the face of adversity became a cornerstone of the Lingayath tradition.

Modern Reflections and Revival
Awareness and Education

- Revisiting History: Modern Lingayath communities are increasingly aware of the historical hardships faced by their ancestors. Efforts are being made to revive and celebrate the rich literary and cultural heritage that was nearly lost during the Kalyan Kranthi period.
- Educational Initiatives: Educational institutions and community programs play a vital role in promoting the teachings of Basavanna and other Sharanas. By incorporating these teachings into the curriculum, the community ensures that the values of equality, devotion, and social justice are instilled in the younger generation.

Community Programs

- Celebrating Vachanas: Festivals, literary events, and community gatherings dedicated to the recitation and discussion of Vachanas help keep the teachings alive. These events serve as a reminder of the profound wisdom and progressive ideals that form the foundation of Lingayatism.
- Promoting Inclusivity: Community leaders and spiritual heads actively promote inclusivity and social equality, reinforcing the core tenets of Basava Dharma. Public

statements and initiatives against caste-based practices and discrimination help steer the community towards a more harmonious and equitable existence.

Conclusion

The tragic events of the Kalyan Kranthi period underscore the resilience and unwavering faith of the Lingayath community. Despite the destruction of their literary heritage and the severe persecution they faced, the Sharanas succeeded in preserving their teachings and principles. By continuing to adhere to the core tenets of Basava Dharma, the Lingayath community can reclaim its glory and serve as a beacon of progressive thought and inclusive spirituality.

Preservation of Teachings and Resilience of the Lingayath Community

The Lingayath community faced significant hardships during the Kalyan Kranthi period, which led to the destruction of their rich literary heritage and forced migration. Despite these adversities, the community exhibited remarkable resilience and determination in preserving their teachings and cultural identity.

Preservation of Teachings

Oral Tradition

• Passing Down Knowledge: Many teachings and Vachana poems were preserved through oral tradition. Devotees memorized these spiritual and philosophical texts and passed them down from one generation to the next. This practice ensured that the core principles and wisdom of the Lingayat saints remained intact, even in the absence of written records.

Migration to Safe Havens

- Seeking Refuge: The Sharanas, including prominent figures like Channabasavanna and Akkamahadevi, sought refuge in safer regions such as Ulavi in the Western Ghats and Shrishaila in Andhra Pradesh. These places became centers for the preservation and continuation of their teachings. The natural isolation and protective environment of these regions provided a sanctuary where the community could rebuild and thrive.

Community Support

- Mutual Aid: During these difficult times, the Lingayath community supported each other, helping to maintain their religious practices and cultural identity despite external pressures. The sense of solidarity and mutual aid within the community played a crucial role in their survival and resilience.

Impact on Literature
Loss and Survival

- Destruction of Manuscripts: The forced migration and persecution led to the destruction of many original manuscripts and Vachana poems. This loss was a profound tragedy, as these texts contained invaluable spiritual and philosophical insights.
- Efforts to Preserve: Despite the destruction, some Vachanas survived through the efforts of dedicated followers who memorized and later transcribed them. These followers played a vital role in preserving the

literary heritage of Lingayatism.

Continued Influence

- Inspiring Future Generations: The surviving literature continued to inspire future generations and played a crucial role in the revival of Lingayat traditions and practices. The profound messages of equality, devotion, and social justice found in the Vachanas remained a guiding light for the community.

Legacy
Modern Revival

- Renewed Interest: In recent times, there has been a renewed interest in Lingayath history and literature. Efforts to preserve and promote their rich cultural heritage have gained momentum, ensuring that the teachings of Basavanna and other Sharanas are not forgotten.
- Cultural Heritage: The renewed focus on cultural heritage includes the restoration of historical sites, the publication of preserved texts, and the organization of events celebrating Lingayat traditions.

Educational Institutions

- Promoting Principles: Various educational institutions and organizations have been established to study and teach the principles of Lingayatism. These institutions ensure that the teachings of Basavanna and other Sharanas are passed on to future generations.

- Curriculum Integration: The principles of equality, inclusivity, and devotion are integrated into the curriculum, fostering a deep understanding of Lingayat values among students.

Conclusion

The resilience and determination of the Lingayath community in preserving their teachings and cultural heritage despite the hardships they faced is truly inspiring. Their ability to adapt and persevere in the face of adversity has ensured the survival and revival of their rich spiritual traditions.

The Modern Revival of Lingayath History and Literature

The modern revival of Lingayath history and literature has been driven by a renewed interest in preserving and promoting the rich cultural heritage of the community. Here are some key aspects of this revival:

Educational Institutions

Lingayat Institutions

- Establishment of Schools and Universities: Numerous educational institutions and organizations have been established to study and teach the principles of Lingayatism. These institutions play a crucial role in preserving and promoting Lingayath history and literature. For example, KLE Society and BLDE Association have set up a network of schools, colleges, and research centers dedicated to educational excellence and cultural preservation.
- Role of Research Centers: Dedicated research centers focus on studying Lingayath history, philosophy, and literature. They provide a platform for scholars to delve into the rich cultural heritage and produce valuable

academic work that sheds light on various aspects of Lingayatism.

Research and Publications

- Active Scholarship: Scholars and researchers are actively involved in studying and publishing works on Lingayath history, philosophy, and literature. This scholarly activity helps bring more attention to the community's rich cultural heritage. For instance, comprehensive studies on Vachana literature have been published, making these works accessible to a wider audience.
- Dissemination of Knowledge: Publications of research findings and historical studies ensure that the teachings and contributions of Lingayat saints are preserved for future generations. These publications often include translations, commentaries, and analyses that make the original texts more comprehensible to contemporary readers.

Cultural Organizations
Cultural Festivals

- Celebration of Traditions: Lingayath cultural festivals and events are organized to celebrate and promote their traditions and heritage. Festivals such as Basava Jayanti, which commemorates the birth anniversary of Basavanna, provide a platform for the community to come together and showcase their cultural practices. These events feature recitations of Vachanas, cultural performances, and community gatherings that foster a sense of unity and pride.

- Promotion of Arts and Literature: Cultural festivals often include exhibitions, competitions, and workshops that promote the arts and literature associated with Lingayatism. These activities help to engage the younger generation and ensure the continuation of cultural traditions.

Community Support

- Organizational Efforts: Various cultural organizations and community groups work towards preserving Lingayath traditions and promoting their teachings. These organizations often organize events, workshops, and seminars to educate people about Lingayath history and literature. For example, the Basava Samithi and other similar organizations play an active role in community outreach and cultural promotion.
- Workshops and Seminars: Regular workshops and seminars are conducted to educate the community about the philosophical and cultural tenets of Lingayatism. These educational initiatives help to reinforce the community's understanding of their heritage and encourage active participation in cultural preservation.

Digital Preservation
Online Archives

- Digitization Efforts: Efforts have been made to digitize and preserve Lingayath literature and historical documents. Online archives and digital libraries provide access to these resources, making them available to a wider audience. Platforms such as the Digital Library of India and specific Lingayat community websites host digitized versions of Vachanas, historical texts, and scholarly articles.

- Global Accessibility: Digital preservation efforts ensure that valuable cultural and historical resources are accessible to people worldwide. This accessibility helps to raise awareness about Lingayath heritage and promotes cross-cultural understanding.

Social Media

- Raising Awareness: Social media platforms are used to share information about Lingayath history and literature. This has helped in reaching a global audience and raising awareness about the community's rich cultural heritage. Pages and groups dedicated to Lingayatism on platforms like Facebook, Twitter, and YouTube provide a space for discussion, education, and community engagement.
- Engaging the Youth: Social media initiatives engage the younger generation by using modern communication tools to share historical facts, religious teachings, and cultural events. This engagement helps to bridge the gap between traditional teachings and contemporary lifestyles.

Revival of Vachana Sahitya
Vachana Literature

- Renewed Interest: There has been a renewed interest in Vachana literature, with efforts to translate and publish these works in modern languages. This has made Vachana poetry more accessible to contemporary readers and scholars. The translation of Vachanas into English, Hindi, and other languages has expanded their reach and impact.

- Academic Courses: Some universities and colleges offer courses on Vachana literature and Lingayath history, providing students with an opportunity to study these subjects in depth. These courses often include critical analysis, historical context, and philosophical exploration of the Vachanas.

Academic Courses

- In-depth Study: Universities and academic institutions offer specialized courses on Lingayatism, Vachana literature, and the historical contributions of Lingayat saints. These courses provide students with comprehensive knowledge and encourage scholarly research in these fields.

Influence on Modern Society
Social Reforms

- Inspirational Principles: The principles of Lingayathism, such as social equality and personal spiritual development, continue to inspire social reforms and movements in modern society. Activists and reformers draw on the teachings of Basavanna and other saints to address contemporary issues such as caste discrimination, gender inequality, and social injustice.
- Community Initiatives: Lingayat principles are reflected in community initiatives that promote social welfare, education, and healthcare. These initiatives align with the values of Dasoha (selfless service) and Kayaka

(work as worship).

Cultural Identity

- Strengthening Identity: The revival of Lingayath history and literature has helped the community strengthen its cultural identity and preserve its unique traditions and practices. By reconnecting with their historical roots, Lingayats are able to foster a sense of pride and belonging.
- Cultural Pride: Celebrating and promoting Lingayath heritage instills a sense of pride within the community and encourages the preservation of cultural practices for future generations.

Conclusion

The modern revival of Lingayath history and literature is a testament to the resilience and determination of the community to preserve and promote their rich cultural heritage. Through the efforts of educational institutions, cultural organizations, digital platforms, and dedicated individuals, the teachings and traditions of Lingayatism continue to thrive and inspire.

Basavanna: A Visionary Social Reformer and Advocate for Democracy

Social Equality and Inclusivity

Opposition to Discrimination

- Challenging Caste, Class, and Gender Discrimination: Basavanna strongly opposed caste, class, and gender discrimination. He envisioned a society where everyone, regardless of their background, had equal opportunities and rights. This principle of social equality is a cornerstone of democratic values.
- Inclusive Society: By advocating for the dismantling of social hierarchies, Basavanna laid the foundation for a more inclusive society. His teachings continue to inspire efforts to promote equality and social justice.

Anubhava Mantapa
Platform for Open Dialogue

- Establishment of Anubhava Mantapa: Basavanna established the Anubhava Mantapa, a spiritual and philosophical forum where people from all walks of life could come together to discuss and share their spiritual experiences. This inclusive approach promoted open dialogue and democratic participation, allowing voices from diverse backgrounds to be heard.
- Model for Modern Forums: The Anubhava Mantapa serves as a model for contemporary forums that promote inclusive dialogue and democratic engagement. It exemplifies the importance of open communication and collective decision-making in a democratic society.

Empowerment of Women
Advocacy for Gender Equality

- Championing Women's Rights: Basavanna was a strong advocate for women's rights and empowerment. He recognized the importance of women's identity and rights, and encouraged their participation in spiritual and social activities. This emphasis on gender equality aligns with democratic principles of equal rights for all.

- Inclusive Participation: By promoting the active involvement of women in all aspects of life, Basavanna challenged the patriarchal norms of his time and paved the way for greater gender equality.

Rejection of Rituals and Superstitions
Rational Approach to Spirituality

- Critique of Ritualistic Practices: Basavanna rejected meaningless rituals and superstitions, advocating for a more rational and spiritual approach to life. His teachings emphasized personal spiritual development and ethical living, which are essential components of a just and democratic society.
- Focus on Inner Devotion: By prioritizing inner devotion and ethical conduct over external rituals, Basavanna promoted a form of spirituality that is accessible and meaningful to all individuals, regardless of their social status.

Democratic Social Structure
Vision of an Inclusive Society

- Promotion of Equal Opportunities: Basavanna envisioned the establishment of a democratic social structure as his ultimate goal. He promoted equal opportunities for all and encouraged the use of local languages in both secular and spiritual education. This emphasis on cultural and linguistic diversity is a key aspect of democratic principles.

- Cultural and Linguistic Inclusivity: By advocating for the use of local languages and cultural practices, Basavanna ensured that education and spiritual teachings were accessible to everyone, fostering a more inclusive and democratic society.

Legacy
Inspiration for Modern Movements

- Continuing Influence: Basavanna's teachings continue to inspire movements for social justice and equality. His emphasis on inclusivity, ethical living, and personal spiritual development resonates with democratic values and continues to influence contemporary society.
- Enduring Vision: Basavanna's vision of an inclusive and just society remains relevant and inspiring today. His contributions to social equality and democratic principles have made him a pioneer in the history of social reform.

Basavanna's contributions to social equality and democratic principles have made him a pioneering figure in the history of social reform. His vision of an inclusive and just society continues to inspire and guide modern efforts towards social justice and equality.

Global Recognition
Statue in London

- Symbol of Global Recognition: The statue of Basaveshwara in London symbolizes his global recognition and the alignment of his teachings with democratic values. It serves as a powerful reminder of his contributions to social equality and justice.

- Significance: Located near the British Parliament on the bank of the River Thames at Albert Embankment, the statue commemorates Basaveshwara's legacy as a 12th-century Indian philosopher, social reformer, and pioneer of democratic principles. The statue was unveiled on November 14, 2015, by the then Prime Minister of India, Shri Narendra Modi. This event highlights the global resonance of Basaveshwara's ideas.
- Inscriptions and Reliefs: The statue features inscriptions that emphasize Basaveshwara's core values of freedom of speech, respect, and tolerance. The plinth includes deep relief scenes depicting significant moments from Basaveshwara's life, showcasing his journey as a social reformer.

CHAPTER TWENTY-EIGHT

Basavanna: Resonance with Gen Z, Digital Activism, and Social Justice:

Basavanna's teachings are increasingly relevant to GenZ due to their emphasis on social equality, ethical living, and personal spiritual development. Here are some ways in which his teachings resonate with the younger generation:

Social Equality and Inclusivity
Alignment with Modern Values

- Strong Stance Against Discrimination: Basavanna's strong stance against caste and gender discrimination aligns with the modern values of equality and inclusivity. Young people today are passionate about social justice and equality, and Basavanna's teachings provide a historical foundation for these ideals.

- Inspiration for Social Movements: His advocacy for the rights of all individuals, regardless of their social status, continues to inspire contemporary movements for social justice, empowering the younger generation to challenge discrimination and promote inclusivity.

Ethical Living
Resonance with Modern Ethos

- Emphasis on Honest Labor: Basavanna's emphasis on ethical living and honest labor resonates with the younger generation's desire for authenticity and integrity. In a world where ethical consumerism and corporate responsibility are gaining importance, his teachings on ethical trade and community service are highly relevant.
- Modern Applications: His principles encourage young people to engage in professions and activities that align with ethical values, promoting a culture of responsibility and integrity in both personal and professional life.

Personal Spiritual Development
Encouraging Introspective Paths

- Focus on Personal Growth: The focus on personal spiritual development and direct communion with the divine appeals to those seeking a more personal and introspective spiritual path. Basavanna's concept of the Ishtalinga, a personal symbol of Shiva, encourages individuals to find their own spiritual path and inner peace.
- Relevance to Spiritual Seekers: This emphasis on inner devotion and personal spiritual growth resonates with the younger generation's quest for meaningful and individualized spiritual experiences.

Community Engagement
Model for Modern Engagement

- Anubhava Mantapa: Basavanna's establishment of the Anubhava Mantapa, a forum for open dialogue and spiritual exchange, is a model for modern community engagement. Young people today value open discussions and inclusive platforms where diverse voices can be heard and respected.
- Promoting Inclusivity: The concept of Anubhava Mantapa inspires contemporary forums and community organizations that foster inclusive dialogue, collective decision-making, and mutual respect.

Environmental Consciousness
Harmony with Nature

- Teachings on Nature: Basavanna's teachings on living harmoniously with nature and respecting all forms of life resonate with the growing environmental consciousness among the younger generation. His emphasis on simplicity and sustainability aligns with contemporary efforts to protect the environment.
- Modern Relevance: His principles support eco-friendly practices and encourage a sustainable lifestyle that values environmental stewardship.

Cultural Preservation
Revival of Heritage

- Vachana Literature: The revival of Basavanna's Vachana literature and his teachings on social equality and ethical living are part of broader efforts to preserve and promote cultural heritage. Young people are increasingly interested in learning about their cultural roots and finding ways to integrate traditional wisdom into modern life.

- Educational and Cultural Initiatives: Efforts to preserve and celebrate Basavanna's literary contributions through educational programs and cultural events help strengthen the community's cultural identity and ensure the transmission of these values to future generations.

Basavanna's teachings and legacy continue to inspire individuals and communities worldwide. His vision of a just and inclusive society remains relevant and powerful, encouraging us to strive for equality, ethical living, and democratic values. By integrating his principles into contemporary life, we can work towards building a more equitable and compassionate world.

Global Influence
Resonance Beyond India

- Influencing Global Movements: Basavanna's teachings have found resonance far beyond India, influencing global movements for social equality and ethical living. His message of inclusivity and personal spiritual development has universal appeal, inspiring individuals and communities worldwide.
- Universal Message: The principles of equality, justice, and rationality espoused by Basavanna transcend geographical boundaries. His teachings inspire people to pursue social justice and personal spiritual growth on a global scale.

Statue in London

- Symbol of Global Recognition: The statue of Basaveshwara in London symbolizes his global recognition and the alignment of his teachings with democratic values. It stands as a powerful reminder of his contributions to social equality and justice.
- Significance: Located near the British Parliament on the bank of the River Thames at Albert Embankment, the statue was unveiled on November 14, 2015, by the then Prime Minister of India, Shri Narendra Modi. This event underscores the global resonance of Basaveshwara's ideas and highlights the universal relevance of his principles.
- Inscriptions and Reliefs: The statue features inscriptions that emphasize Basaveshwara's core values of freedom of speech, respect, and tolerance. The plinth includes deep relief scenes depicting significant moments from Basaveshwara's life, showcasing his journey as a social reformer and philosopher.

Basavanna: Relevance to Generation 2000+

Basavanna's teachings are becoming increasingly relevant to Generation 2000+ due to their emphasis on social equality, ethical living, and personal spiritual development. Here are some ways in which his teachings resonate with the younger generation:

Social Equality and Inclusivity

Alignment with Modern Values

- Strong Stance Against Discrimination: Basavanna's strong stance against caste and gender discrimination aligns with the modern values of equality and inclusivity. Young people today are passionate about social justice and equality, and Basavanna's teachings provide a historical foundation for these ideals.

- Inspiration for Social Movements: His advocacy for the rights of all individuals, regardless of their social status, continues to inspire contemporary movements for social justice, empowering the younger generation to challenge discrimination and promote inclusivity.

Ethical Living
Resonance with Modern Ethos

- Emphasis on Honest Labor: Basavanna's emphasis on ethical living and honest labor resonates with the younger generation's desire for authenticity and integrity. In a world where ethical consumerism and corporate responsibility are gaining importance, his teachings on ethical trade and community service are highly relevant.
- Modern Applications: His principles encourage young people to engage in professions and activities that align with ethical values, promoting a culture of responsibility and integrity in both personal and professional life.

Personal Spiritual Development
Encouraging Introspective Paths

- Focus on Personal Growth: The focus on personal spiritual development and direct communion with the divine appeals to those seeking a more personal and introspective spiritual path. Basavanna's concept of the Ishtalinga, a personal symbol of Shiva, encourages individuals to find their own spiritual path and inner peace.

- Relevance to Spiritual Seekers: This emphasis on inner devotion and personal spiritual growth resonates with the younger generation's quest for meaningful and individualized spiritual experiences.

Community Engagement
Model for Modern Engagement

- Anubhava Mantapa: Basavanna's establishment of the Anubhava Mantapa, a forum for open dialogue and spiritual exchange, is a model for modern community engagement. Young people today value open discussions and inclusive platforms where diverse voices can be heard and respected.
- Promoting Inclusivity: The concept of Anubhava Mantapa inspires contemporary forums and community organizations that foster inclusive dialogue, collective decision-making, and mutual respect.

Environmental Consciousness
Harmony with Nature

- Teachings on Nature: Basavanna's teachings on living harmoniously with nature and respecting all forms of life resonate with the growing environmental consciousness among the younger generation. His emphasis on simplicity and sustainability aligns with contemporary efforts to protect the environment.
- Modern Relevance: His principles support eco-friendly practices and encourage a sustainable lifestyle that values environmental stewardship.

Cultural Preservation
Revival of Heritage

- Vachana Literature: The revival of Basavanna's Vachana literature and his teachings on social equality and ethical living are part of broader efforts to preserve and promote cultural heritage. Young people are increasingly interested in learning about their cultural roots and finding ways to integrate traditional wisdom into modern life.

- Educational and Cultural Initiatives: Efforts to preserve and celebrate Basavanna's literary contributions through educational programs and cultural events help strengthen the community's cultural identity and ensure the transmission of these values to future generations.

Digital Age Integration
Ethical Technology and Business Practices

- Corporate Social Responsibility (CSR): Many companies are embracing CSR initiatives, reflecting Basavanna's principles of ethical trade and community service. Businesses are increasingly focusing on sustainable practices, fair trade, and contributing to societal well-being.

- Transparency and Accountability: With the rise of digital platforms, there is a growing emphasis on transparency and accountability in business practices. Companies are using technology to ensure their operations are ethical and transparent, aligning with Basavanna's teachings.

Basavanna's teachings continue to inspire and guide the younger generation, providing a timeless framework for navigating the complexities of modern life while staying true to core values of equality, integrity, and spiritual growth. His visionary ideas on social equality, ethical living, and personal spiritual development remain as relevant and powerful today as they were in the 12th century.

Digital Activism and Social Justice
Online Advocacy

- Raising Awareness: The internet has become a powerful tool for advocating social justice and equality. Young people are leveraging social media and online platforms to raise awareness about social issues, combat discrimination, and promote inclusivity. This echoes Basavanna's vision of social equality and his efforts to create a just society.
- Examples of Success: Campaigns such as #MeToo and #BlackLivesMatter have utilized digital platforms to mobilize support, highlight injustices, and drive social change.

Crowdsourcing and Fundraising

- Supporting Social Causes: Digital platforms enable individuals and organizations to crowdfund for social causes, supporting community projects, educational initiatives, and charitable activities. This modern approach to philanthropy aligns with Basavanna's emphasis on community service and ethical living.

Personal Ethical Living in the Digital Age

Mindful Consumption

- Ethical Choices: People are becoming more conscious about their digital consumption, choosing products and services from companies that align with ethical and sustainable values. This practice reflects Basavanna's teachings on ethical living and responsible consumerism.
- Supporting Ethical Brands: By favoring companies with fair trade practices, sustainable production methods, and ethical labor policies, consumers are advocating for a more just and equitable economy.

Digital Detox and Balance

- Well-being and Balance: There is a growing awareness of the importance of digital well-being. Practices like digital detox, mindfulness, and maintaining a healthy work-life balance are becoming more popular. These practices reflect Basavanna's emphasis on ethical living, personal well-being, and the importance of mental and spiritual health.

E-learning and Digital Education
Access to Knowledge

- Democratizing Education: Online educational platforms provide access to knowledge and learning resources for people from all backgrounds. This democratization of education aligns with Basavanna's vision of equal opportunities for all, regardless of social status or geographic location.

- Examples: Platforms like Coursera, Khan Academy, and edX offer courses that are accessible to a global audience, helping to bridge educational gaps and empower learners.

Promoting Vachana Literature

- Digital Preservation: Digital platforms are used to preserve and promote Vachana literature, making Basavanna's teachings accessible to a global audience. Online courses, e-books, and digital archives help spread his message of ethical living and social equality.
- Cultural Awareness: Projects like digitizing and translating Vachanas contribute to preserving cultural heritage and making it available to contemporary readers worldwide.

Community Building and Virtual Forums
Online Communities

- Virtual Connection: Virtual forums and online communities allow people to connect, share ideas, and support each other, similar to the Anubhava Mantapa. These platforms promote open dialogue, inclusivity, and community engagement.
- Modern Mantapas: Online platforms such as Reddit, Discord, and community-specific forums provide spaces for inclusive discussions on social, philosophical, and spiritual topics.

Digital Volunteering

- Global Outreach: Volunteering opportunities through digital platforms enable people to contribute to social causes from anywhere in the world. This reflects Basavanna's principles of community service and ethical living.
- Examples: Platforms like VolunteerMatch and Idealist connect individuals with volunteer opportunities, allowing them to support causes they are passionate about.

Sustainable Tech Innovations
Green Technology

- Eco-friendly Innovations: Innovations in green technology and sustainable practices in tech development reflect Basavanna's emphasis on harmony with nature and ethical responsibility. Companies are focusing on reducing their carbon footprint and developing eco-friendly products.
- Sustainable Solutions: Examples include the development of renewable energy technologies, sustainable packaging solutions, and initiatives to reduce electronic waste.

By integrating Basavanna's teachings into the digital realm, the younger generation is finding new ways to uphold values of authenticity, integrity, and social equality in the age of technology. This modern adaptation of his principles ensures that his legacy continues to inspire positive change in contemporary society.

About The Author

Chennamallikarjun C. Bhusanur is a seasoned Investigation Professional whose career has been marked by a relentless pursuit of truth and justice. Blessed with a natural inquisitiveness and a keen researching mind, he has authored several acclaimed books on the intricacies of the investigation profession. His work in the field of investigation has been instrumental in unraveling complex cases and establishing a reputation for thoroughness and integrity.

Driven by an eternal inquisitive spirit, Chennamallikarjun has ventured beyond the realm of professional investigations to explore the profound teachings of Lingayatism. His deep-rooted curiosity and passion for understanding the essence of life, dharma, and spirituality have led him to pen this book, merging his free-flowing thinking process with the timeless wisdom of Lingayat philosophy.

In this work, Chennamallikarjun delves into the core principles of Lingayatism and their relevance to modern corporate governance. His unique perspective, shaped by years of investigative rigor and a profound appreciation for Basavanna's teachings, offers readers valuable insights into the intersection of tradition and modernity.

Through this book, Chennamallikarjun invites readers on a journey of continuous learning and personal growth, inspired by the timeless values of social equality, ethical living, and selfless service. His exploration of Lingayatism is not just an academic exercise but a heartfelt quest to understand and apply its principles in everyday life.

With a commitment to living by the ideals of integrity, service, and compassion, Chennamallikarjun C. Bhusanur presents " The Lingayat way: Ethical leadership and Corporate Governance " as a testament to the enduring relevance of ancient wisdom in our contemporary world.

Other Books By Chennamallikarjun C. Bhusanur

1. *"Undercover Chronicles: Insights into Indian Private Detectives" (Notion Press)*

In this compelling and insightful work, Chennamallikarjun C. Bhusanur takes readers on an intriguing journey into the world of Indian private detectives. Drawing from his extensive experience, he provides a fascinating look at the skills, challenges, and dedication required in the field. The book highlights the ingenuity and resourcefulness of investigators as they solve complex cases and bring clarity to intricate situations. It celebrates the profession's crucial role in upholding justice and uncovering truth, making it a must-read for anyone interested in the exciting and dynamic world of private investigations in India.

2. *"Eyes in the Shadow: Your Blueprint for Corporate Dominance" (Notion Press)*

In "Eyes in the Shadow," Chennamallikarjun offers a strategic guide for achieving corporate dominance. The book combines practical advice with real-world examples to help readers navigate the complexities of the corporate landscape. Chennamallikarjun's unique insights into corporate espionage, competitive intelligence, and strategic planning provide readers with the tools they need to outmaneuver competitors and thrive in the business world. This book is an invaluable resource for business leaders, managers, and entrepreneurs seeking to gain a competitive edge.

3. "Claims & Clues: The Art of Insurance Investigation" (Notion Press)

In "Claims & Clues," Chennamallikarjun C. Bhusanur explores the specialized field of insurance investigation. This book provides a comprehensive overview of the techniques and strategies used to uncover fraud, assess claims, and ensure justice in the insurance industry. With detailed case studies and practical advice, Chennamallikarjun demystifies the process of insurance investigation, making it accessible to professionals and novices alike. This book is an essential guide for insurance investigators, claims adjusters, and anyone involved in the insurance industry.